COMPUTATIONAL GLOBAL MACRO

Game Theory,
Machine Learning,
and Causal Inference

COMPUTATIONAL GLOBAL MACRO

Game Theory, Machine Learning, and Causal Inference

Joseph Simonian
Autonomous Investment Technologies, USA

NEW JERSEY · LONDON · SINGAPORE · BEIJING · SHANGHAI · HONG KONG · TAIPEI · CHENNAI · TOKYO

Published by

World Scientific Publishing Co. Pte. Ltd.
5 Toh Tuck Link, Singapore 596224
USA office: 27 Warren Street, Suite 401-402, Hackensack, NJ 07601
UK office: 57 Shelton Street, Covent Garden, London WC2H 9HE

Library of Congress Cataloging-in-Publication Data
Names: Simonian, Joseph, author.
Title: Computational global macro : game theory, machine learning and causal inference / Joseph Simonian, Autonomous Investment Technologies, USA.
Description: New Jersey: World Scientific Publishing Co. Pte. Ltd., [2025] | Includes bibliographical references and index.
Identifiers: LCCN 2024032843 | ISBN 9789811293955 (hardcover) | ISBN 9789811293962 (ebook for institutions) | ISBN 9789811293979 (ebook for individuals)
Subjects: LCSH: Financial risk management--Data processing. | Investments, Foreign--Decision making--Data processing. | Geopolitics--Economic aspects. | Game theory. | Machine learning.
Classification: LCC HD61 .S484 2025 | DDC 332.63/2042--dc23/eng/20240917
LC record available at https://lccn.loc.gov/2024032843

British Library Cataloguing-in-Publication Data
A catalogue record for this book is available from the British Library.

Copyright © 2025 by World Scientific Publishing Co. Pte. Ltd.

All rights reserved. This book, or parts thereof, may not be reproduced in any form or by any means, electronic or mechanical, including photocopying, recording or any information storage and retrieval system now known or to be invented, without written permission from the publisher.

For photocopying of material in this volume, please pay a copying fee through the Copyright Clearance Center, Inc., 222 Rosewood Drive, Danvers, MA 01923, USA. In this case permission to photocopy is not required from the publisher.

For any available supplementary material, please visit
https://www.worldscientific.com/worldscibooks/10.1142/13860#t=suppl

Desk Editors: Balasubramanian Shanmugam/Pui Yee Lum

Typeset by Stallion Press
Email: enquiries@stallionpress.com

Preface

Among non-financial drivers of investment performance, perhaps none is at the forefront of investors' minds more than geopolitical risk. This is due to the fact that markets are governed by institutions that are part of the "connective tissue" of nation-states, which in turn are the primary actors in international affairs. Thus, the interactions of states with one another and important non-state actors can have significant impacts on market performance. The degree to which investment strategies use assessments of geopolitical risk in their investment processes varies. The investment style known as *global macro investing* explicitly incorporates macroeconomic and geopolitical information during the investment decision-making process.

There are two basic types of global macro investing: *discretionary global macro* and *systematic global macro*. Discretionary global macro investing is primarily driven by fundamental or qualitative information. Portfolio management teams that run discretionary strategies will typically try to build expertise in various countries and markets, and will make investment decisions based on macroeconomic and geopolitical analysis. The research process in discretionary macro strategies may include "on-the-ground" conversations with policymakers, business leaders, local economists, and other individuals who the portfolio managers believe have valuable insights with respect to a given market. In contrast, *systematic global macro* funds use data (both historical and real time) and quantitative models to drive their investment decisions. The models can be based on traditional econometrics or machine learning.[1]

This book straddles the middle ground between discretionary and systematic global macro investing. It is primarily concerned with the types of questions addressed by a sub-branch of discretionary global macro investing known as *thematic global macro*, which focuses on geopolitical and macroeconomic developments that are likely to have the broadest impact on financial markets. However, in sympathy with systematic global macro, this book is also focused on providing a more rigorous quantitative foundation for the expression of thematic investment ideas.[2] In particular, we apply the tools of game theory, machine learning, and causal inference to develop an approach we call *computational global macro*.

Given the foregoing, the book can be considered a counterpoint to the standard approach to thematic global macro investing. Many investment firms engaged in thematic global macro investing have large armies of personnel tasked with forming views and writing commentary on current and prospective developments in world affairs. Although there is no lack of research on geopolitical themes and risks, not all of it is equally valuable to investors. The primary failing of much of the geopolitical research that is produced by investment firms is that it often displays a lack of analytical depth and historical context, and it is almost never couched within a systematic, mathematically grounded framework for understanding the dynamics within and among geopolitical actors. Rather, many of the geopolitically oriented pieces that are produced by investment firms often read less like research articles and more like op-ed columns with charts.

Developing high-quality geopolitical analysis is especially challenging today for a number of reasons. The primary reason is that there are so many potentially impactful geopolitical factors that it is difficult to build thoughtful views on all of them, especially given the resource constraints of most firms. This is directly related to the lack of depth we find in many of the pieces of geopolitical research

---

[1] For an application of machine learning to systematic global macro, see Simonian and Wu (2019).

[2] The seeds of this book can be found in the ideas presented in Simonian (2021).

produced by investment firms. Although firms would generally like to chime in on every current event, most are simply not equipped to do so in a coherent manner.

Given the challenges inherent in uncovering and analyzing the sources, dimensions, and potential impacts of geopolitical risk on investment outcomes, in this book, we define and explain the basic dimensions of geopolitical risk as it pertains to portfolio management and then provide a rigorous analytical framework to analyze geopolitical events. While it is beyond the scope of one book to present a comprehensive methodology that covers every aspect of geopolitical risk, it is nevertheless possible to present an approach to analyzing geopolitics that provides more analytical clarity and investment relevance compared to the prevailing approach to geopolitical analysis in the investment industry.

The framework we present in this book has two primary analytical pillars. The first is *game theory*, which lends itself to the detailed *structural* analysis of conflict and cooperation among agents. Game theory is the formal study of strategic interaction and has been used as a tool for geopolitical analysis for decades. Indeed, many famous geopolitical events have been analyzed using game theory. A case in point is the Cuban Missile Crisis in 1962. During this pivotal event, the United States and the Soviet Union were engaged in a strategic game of brinkmanship over the placement of nuclear missiles in Cuba. Each side had to carefully consider its options and potential payoffs while trying to avoid a catastrophic nuclear war. Beyond political-military interactions, game theory can also be applied to analyze situations dealing with economic relations. Consider OPEC (Organization of the Petroleum Exporting Countries), whose members have to balance their own interests in maximizing revenue with the collective interest of the cartel. Each member must carefully consider its production levels and pricing strategies, considering the potential actions of other members. Game theory is thus applicable to the full spectrum of topics that are relevant for global macro managers.

Our particular emphasis is on *computational game theory*, the combination of game theoretic and algorithmic approaches to analyzing decision-making. As such, the second analytical pillar of the book is *machine learning*, especially what is known as *reinforcement learning*, a branch of machine learning that studies how agents learn to maximize rewards in specific environments. By an "environment," we mean a specific state of the world, actions that an agent can take, and rewards and punishments attached to specific actions. Reinforcement learning is premised upon the idea that agents learn based on experiences that give them rewards or punishments in a given state and based on the pattern of rewards and punishments experienced in previous states. As they learn, agents are able to make more informed decisions in the future. Moreover, in some environments, they are able to influence the state by their actions. Rewards and punishments ("carrots and sticks") are of course an important component of geopolitical interaction. They are also important dimensions of game theoretic analysis. Therefore, there are fundamental points of overlap between international relations, reinforcement learning, and game theory. By combining game theoretical methods with sophisticated computational techniques, we show how to build simulations that will give investors the ability to construct detailed scenario analyses of prospective geopolitical events. In doing so, we hope to bring new depth to the analysis of geopolitics for macro investors.

The layout of this book is as follows. Chapter 1 discusses theories of human rationality and international affairs. While our aim in this book is to provide a quantitative basis for thematic global macro investing, we believe that it is nevertheless important for investors to couch their models within robust conceptual frameworks. Our intent is not to promote any particular theoretical construct but to provide investors with the background knowledge that will enable them to form their own coherent geopolitical worldviews. This will in turn allow them to build theoretically sound models.

After providing the conceptual building blocks needed to conduct geopolitical analysis, we present a wide variety of quantitative models that can be used to simulate interactions between international actors. Chapter 2 is devoted to analyzing how game theory and reinforcement learning can be used to model conflict between agents. Various game structures are presented and married to a class of reinforcement learning algorithms known as *contextual multi-armed bandit* (CMAB) models, which allow us to model and simulate non-cooperative interaction over multiple periods. The antithesis of conflict, of course, is cooperation, which we discuss in Chapter 3. In analyzing cooperative interaction, we also utilize CMAB models as well as a model known as the *Gale–Shapley algorithm* to investigate how agents can successfully bring about collective action to achieve commonly held goals.

Strategic interaction depends intimately on the ability of agents to learn over time in complex environments. Chapter 4 is accordingly devoted to an analysis of a new set of more sophisticated games. To facilitate the discussion, the chapter introduces a new reinforcement learning framework, *Q-learning*, which is a type of reinforcement learning algorithm that assumes that agents' actions can influence the state of the world they are in during successive rounds of interaction. Q-learning thus differs from CMAB-type frameworks in which agents are not able to influence the state they are in through their actions. Through numerous examples, we show readers how to apply Q-learning to games with more complex dynamics.

Another important dimension of strategic interaction encompasses the *causal relations* that drive conflict and cooperation. Analyzing causal relations in the geopolitical realm is important in order to gain a clear understanding of the sources and ultimate effects of global developments. Surprisingly, rigorous methods for causal inference have not been widely adopted by many quantitative investors, although that is beginning to change.[3] Chapter 5 is devoted to this topic. We describe some of the most widely used statistical tools of causal inference and how they can be brought to bear on geopolitical analysis in combination with game theory and reinforcement learning or as standalone tools. This chapter also introduces the *SARSA* and *Thompson Sampling* algorithms.

Developing sound geopolitical and macroeconomic views is critical to thematic global macro investing. However, simply having views is not enough. Investors need a way to express their views in actual portfolios. Accordingly, Chapter 6, the final chapter of the book, is devoted to discussing portfolio construction techniques. We begin by showing how linear programming techniques can be adapted to processing directional views based on geopolitical, macro, and causal considerations. We then describe the quadratic programming-based method of mean–variance optimization and its Bayesian extension in the Black–Litterman model. Because thematic views are often

---

[3]See, for instance, Simonian (2021, 2022, 2023) and De Prado (2023).

expressed on a relative ordinal basis (e.g., "the US market will perform better than the Japanese market"), we also introduce a version of the Black–Litterman model that allows investors to express their views on returns, variances, and covariances in the form of ranks.

One of the critical aspects of portfolio management is model validation. The fundamental way in which a model is validated is by testing its robustness under different market scenarios. A number of techniques for model validation, such as Monte Carlo simulation and bootstrapping, are well known to the investment community. In Chapter 6, we introduce a less familiar yet no-less-effective approach to model validation based on a machine learning framework called Generative Adversarial Networks (GANs). By using GANs, investors can generate synthetic market data with different characteristics, which can then be used to build robust portfolios that are more likely to perform well in a multitude of market environments.

We close Chapter 6 with a discussion of collective decision-making in portfolio management teams. This is an important topic given the fact that most portfolios are managed by more than one individual. Our discussion centers on the presentation of a novel framework for aggregating the complex probabilistic judgments that portfolio managers often use as inputs into their decision-making process. The framework we introduce is an adaptation of a solution concept from cooperative game theory known as the *Shapley value*. As we demonstrate, the framework we present not only allows for the probabilistically coherent aggregation of sophisticated chains of reasoning but does so in a manner that is consistent with fundamental notions of rationality.

The intent of this book is to introduce a set of concepts and tools to investment professionals, academics, and students that they have not likely encountered before. While numerous examples are presented and discussed in detail, ideally, readers will use the examples as springboards to develop their own more application-specific models. Ultimately, we believe that this book will provide an indispensable guide for any macro investor interested in injecting a heightened level of rigor into their analysis of geopolitical processes and events.

References

López de Prado M. 2023. *Causal Factor Investing: Can Factor Investing Become Scientific?* Cambridge: Cambridge University Press.

Simonian, J. and Wu, C. 2019. Minsky vs. Machine: New foundations for quant-macro investing. *The Journal of Financial Data Science* 1(2): 94–110.

Simonian, J. 2021a. Geopolitical risk in investment research: allies, adversaries, and algorithms. *The Journal of Portfolio Management* 47(9): 92–109.

Simonian, J. 2021b. Causal uncertainty in capital markets: A robust Noisy-OR framework for portfolio management. *The Journal of Financial Data Science* 3(1): 43–55.

Simonian, J. 2022. Investment decisions under almost complete causal ignorance. *The Journal of Portfolio Management* 49(1): 33–38.

Simonian, J. 2023. A causal analysis of market contagion: A double machine learning approach. *The Journal of Financial Data Science* 5(2): 9–22.

About the Author

Joseph Simonian is a globally renowned investor and researcher who has conducted extensive research in quantitative finance, machine learning, factor investing, and portfolio construction. Over the course of a 20-year career in the investment industry, Joseph has held senior portfolio management and research positions in several prominent asset management firms and institutions. Joseph is a noted contributor to leading finance journals and is also a prominent speaker at investment events worldwide. He is currently the co-editor of the *Journal of Financial Data Science* and is also on the editorial board of *The Journal of Portfolio Management*. Joseph has authored over 40 publications in leading investment journals. He is also the co-author of the book *Quantitative Global Bond Portfolio Management*. In addition to his portfolio management and research activities, Joseph also has extensive experience teaching in both academia and industry. He holds a Ph.D. from the University of California, Santa Barbara; an M.A. from Columbia University; and a B.A. from the University of California, Los Angeles.

Contents

Preface   v

About the Author   xiii

1. **Theories of Human Rationality and International Relations**   1
   - 1.1 Global Cooperation and Conflict as Collective Action Problems 1
   - 1.2 Painting a Realistic Picture of Human Rationality . . 3
   - 1.3 The Role of Commitments in International Relations 5
   - 1.4 The Origin of Cooperation 6
   - 1.5 Social Norms, Social Roles, and Reciprocity 9
   - 1.6 Rational Agency in International Affairs 14
   - 1.7 Concluding Points 20
   - References 20

2. **Conflict**   23
   - 2.1 Introduction 23
   - 2.2 Agent Preferences 23
   - 2.3 Game Theory Basics 24
   - 2.4 The Prisoner's Dilemma 25
     - 2.4.1 External and Internal Solutions to the Prisoner's Dilemma 28

	2.4.2 The Role of Norms in Solving the Prisoner's Dilemma	32
2.5	Intermezzo: Absolute or Relative Payoffs?	34
2.6	Games of Conflict Beyond the Prisoner's Dilemma	35
2.7	Analyzing Games Using Contextual Multi-Armed Bandits	37
2.8	Simulating Iterated Games Using CMABs	40
2.9	Concluding Points	45
	References	45

3. Cooperation — 47

3.1	The Problem of Coordination	47
3.2	The Origin of Cooperation II: Evidence from Nature	50
3.3	Modeling Cooperative Games Using CMABs	55
3.4	Determining Whether an Agreement Is Fair	59
3.5	Stable Cooperative Structures	62
3.6	Guided Cooperation: Correlated Equilibrium	66
3.7	Concluding Points	69
	References	69

4. Games with Complex Interaction — 71

4.1	Learning in International Relations	71
4.2	Q-learning	72
4.3	The War of Attrition	74
4.4	Signaling Games	77
4.5	Stackelberg Games	81
4.6	Pursuit–Evasion Games	85
4.7	Games with Lexicographic Beliefs	89
4.8	Concluding Points	93
	References	93

5. Causal Inference in Models of Strategic Interaction — 95

5.1	The Problem of Causality	95
5.2	Causal Inference	100
	5.2.1 The *do* Operator	101
5.3	Causal Reinforcement Learning	106

5.4	The Noisy-OR Model	111
5.5	Strategic Decision-making Under Causal Ignorance	119
	5.5.1 A Causal Case Study	120
5.6	Concluding Points	125
References		125

6. Portfolio Construction — 129

6.1	The Final Piece of the Puzzle	129
6.2	Linear Programming	131
	6.2.1 Expressing Causal Views in Portfolios	132
6.3	Quadratic Programming	134
	6.3.1 Mean–Variance Optimization	134
	6.3.2 The Black–Litterman Model	135
	6.3.3 Ordinal Black–Litterman	136
6.4	Robust Optimization	138
	6.4.1 Robust Optimization Using Machine Learning	142
6.5	Judgment Aggregation	148
	6.5.1 Forming Collective Views	151
6.6	Concluding Points	154
References		154

Index — 159

Chapter 1

Theories of Human Rationality and International Relations

1.1 Global Cooperation and Conflict as Collective Action Problems

This book is an effort to provide investors with the tools to conduct high-quality research in international relations and political economy that will hopefully inform their investment decision-making around geopolitical themes. Before introducing the mathematical theory of games in Chapter 2, however, it is first necessary to gain an appreciation for the conceptual and empirical research that has helped shed light on the primary drivers of human behavior in strategic contexts. Gaining an appreciation of the latter research will undoubtedly help us build better formal models of global cooperation and conflict.

Cooperation and conflict are different solutions to the problem of collective action, and both derive from agents' consideration of the following two questions: (1) "Should we cooperate?" and if so, (2) "How do we cooperate?" When cooperation fails, it is customary to explain the problem in terms of utility maximization, maintaining that the problem emerges from the clash between individual and collective rationality at the moment of action and that it is individual rationality that triumphs. Collective rationality is, according to this view, reducible to the set of individual interests that exist within a given group of agents.

However, even if one subscribes to the foregoing conception of collective rationality, two realities should nevertheless be acknowledged. First, maximizing *synchronic* (shorter-term) utility is not always the best strategy for an individual over the long run. Coordination with others often entails the maximization of *diachronic* (longer-term) utility, where short-term sacrifices may be made in order to secure longer-term gains. The creation of military alliances is one example of cooperation whose aim is diachronic utility. The formation of businesses is another. Indeed, most businesses incur losses during the first few years of operations. The principals of any venture know that such losses are a real possibility but are nevertheless willing to absorb them in order to secure future gains. Thus, business activity is primarily concerned with diachronic gain. The second reality of rationality that must be acknowledged is that, rather than engaging in conscious and original deliberation before each decision, much of human action, especially cooperation, is driven by conformity to rules, habits, and conventions.

The importance of rules, habits, and conventions as drivers of human behavior is often lost on investors who deal primarily with numerical data (e.g., time series) that precludes such information. Nevertheless, to successfully analyze geopolitics, we must appreciate that in any social group, the creation of collective order consists in the selection and maintenance of rules that function as coordinating mechanisms for individual behavior. In this respect, financial markets are no different from governments or any other institution. Rules offer a means by which investors' actions can coexist harmoniously. Rules encourage cooperation, which generally ends up benefiting both individual investors and the market as a whole.

Despite the existence of rules, however, it is readily observable that both individual and collective agents fail to cooperate even in situations when doing so would benefit them. A well-known example of cooperation breakdown is what is known as the *free-rider problem* in the production of public goods. Public goods are distinguished from private goods in that they exhibit *jointness* and *non-excludability*. Jointness refers to the ability of a good, once it is produced for one person, to be consumed by more people at no additional cost. Non-excludability refers to the impossibility of excluding certain people from using the good once it is produced. Some examples of public goods include street lighting, public parks, and national defense.

When public good provision is viewed from the individual point of view, there is a great incentive to defect from the production of a public good yet nevertheless benefit from it once it is produced. This is what is known as the *free-rider problem*. If everybody in a group acted as a free rider, very little if any of the public good would be supplied to the group as a whole. If a wholly self-interested individual can defect without threatening the provision of the public good, he or she will likely take advantage of others' efforts at providing it.

How much each person contributes to the provision of a public good will generally hinge on how much he or she believes others will contribute. The more others contribute, the smaller one's contribution will typically be, as long as their free-riding behavior does not jeopardize the provision of the good. For example, consider a community fundraising drive organized to collect funds to provide for a new gymnasium for the local school. In such a situation, a certain threshold must be reached if the public good is to be provided. If, for example, it is somehow revealed that a few large donors will contribute enough funds to fully pay for the construction of the gymnasium, others in the community will have a strong incentive to refrain from contributing anything, as their free riding will not endanger the provision of the gymnasium. Thus, without the threat of punitive action from an external actor, rational egoists will generally provide public goods at suboptimal levels so long as their suboptimal contributions do not completely sabotage the provision of the good. In international affairs, free riding is also common, and both state and non-state actors must take precautions to ensure that their contributions to collective endeavors are not exploited by their partners. In Chapter 2, we will further explore free riding in the context of game theory.

1.2 Painting a Realistic Picture of Human Rationality

The model of rationality that is utilized in game theory, at least in the base case, characterizes agents as perfectly rational self-interested maximizers. While this description is useful for building simplified frameworks of human behavior, it is not an accurate description of either *homo economicus* or *homo politicus*. Indeed, its faithfulness as a model of human rationality has been questioned by many.

One of the skeptics of the maximization view of human rationality has been Herbert Simon (1957), who described the relevant characteristics of a social system in the following way: (1) the properties of a system itself influence its behavior only to the extent that they limit the perfection of its adaptation to the environment; (2) there may be limits both to a system's ability to compute what the rational behavior is in a situation and its ability to carry out the behavior computed. A long-neglected aspect of social science inquiry, Simon claimed, has been the study of the limits of human computational ability and how these limits influence rational action. The focus of standard (neoclassical) economic theory, for example, is choosing among a set of alternatives based on a fixed utility function. However, standard theory does not explain the source of the alternatives or how individuals connect the alternatives to their consequences. Simon found these points important to understanding and predicting real-world behavior. Simon argued that the idea of *bounded rationality* accounts for behavior that traditional economic theory neglects while nevertheless staying in harmony with it, as it is still a type of instrumental ("means-end") rationality. The insertion of cognitive limitations into the standard theory of expected utility ultimately led Simon to claim that boundedly rational agents are best viewed as *satisficers*, accepting any decision whose results in the case at hand are "good enough."

A satisficer is similar to another type of agent, the *constrained maximizer*. The latter concept has been explored in detail by David Gauthier (1986). Like the pure maximizer, the constrained maximizer is driven by instrumental rationality, but his deliberative process differs from that of the pure maximizer in an important way. The constrained maximizer chooses an action not solely on the basis of its optimality but also on the basis of such considerations as the constraints it is bound by, a decision's compatibility with long-term plans and goals, and importantly, the commitments the individual has made. With regard to constraints, it is important to note that they can be internally imposed, as in the case of commitments, or externally imposed, as in the case of social customs and norms; they can be voluntary, as in the case of commitments, or involuntary, as in the case of cognitive constraints.

All decision-makers, including investors, must determine the extent of rational search, i.e., how much information they should consider before an ultimate decision is made. The decision-maker stops searching when the benefit of finding a better option is equal to or less than the costs of further search. The satisficer searches only until finding a choice whose outcomes are good enough. By satisficing with respect to the particular decision at hand, the satisficer saves time and other resources that may then be expended on other decisions. Both satisficing and constrained maximization are different ways of pursuing the same larger goal. Both strategies rest on an implicit recognition that to do what is locally best may not be globally best. Both strategies aim to maximize globally and may prescribe the decision-maker to act in ways that are less than maximally best with respect to the local decision at hand. Both procedures appeal to the idea that a decision-maker who considers less than the full set of factors that bear on a particular decision may for a variety of reasons do better, over a set of decisions, than the maximizer.

In Gauthier's characterization of constrained maximization, agents are inclined to comply with mutually advantageous commitments, provided they get similar compliance from others. Unlike a pure maximizer or satisficer, the constrained maximizer has internalized principles that govern his choices, and in cooperative contexts, he may do better than an agent whose goal is simply to exploit others. Indeed, two constrained maximizers when given the choice between cooperation and conflict, will often choose cooperation if they know that the other has a cooperative inclination because of their respective commitments or adherence to notions of reciprocity, collective welfare, and/or fairness.

1.3 The Role of Commitments in International Relations

Commitment is an idea that is difficult to conceptualize within theories of expected utility because of the assumption that self-interested maximization is the overarching goal of every agent. This is a consequentialist notion where actions amount to a means to achieve some desired end. Acts of commitment are not fundamentally consequentialist because they are presumably carried out independently of the envisaged consequences of the action.

When a commitment is expressed from the first-person point of view in the form of an "I will x" statement, the individual takes responsibility for producing the decision that he is committed to, but also acknowledges that he will be responsible for the decision in the future. That is, by acknowledging that an individual is responsible for a decision that has been made, the individual is agreeing to act within the praxiological constraints set by the decision. It is nevertheless possible that acting on the basis of a commitment may coincide with the maximization of personal welfare. Commitment does not necessarily draw on moral motives, and any number of individual, moral, or cultural drivers can give individuals a source from which their commitments may be drawn. Moreover, one of the ways in which group identity can emerge is through making members of a community accept certain rules of conduct as part of compulsory behavior toward others in the collective. It is not a matter of asking each time, "what do I get out of it?" but of assuming that certain types of behavior toward others are mandatory.

Sen (1977, 1985, 2002) argued that social identification with others presupposes emotional distance from those with whom one identifies. It does so because commitment to others takes the form of an appreciation of the inherent value of the rules at work in the group one is a member of. Commitment is thus not a passionate connection to others, but rather a rational acknowledgment of the rules connected to group membership. Only individuals who have distanced themselves from their own interests can achieve this acknowledgment. In the context of international relations, commitments also function in this manner, especially in the formation and maintenance of alliances. Accordingly, formally accounting for, and incorporating, ideas of commitment in the game theoretic and computational analysis of geopolitical interaction is an important aspect of the model-building process.

1.4 The Origin of Cooperation

As discussed, contemporary social science, especially economics, presents a picture of human rationality that is descriptively inaccurate. We have identified three shortcomings of this picture which are important to explaining what motivates action on the part of individuals: (1) Human reason is bounded, something which constrains individuals' ability to maximize. (2) It is often diachronic, leading individuals to eschew present gains for future ones. (3) It is often non-instrumental in the sense that individuals' desires do not always serve as the prime motivators of action. Now, while (3) is undoubtedly true, it is nevertheless a fact that an important motivator for most individuals engaging in any action, even cooperative action, is the belief that their actions bring direct benefits to them individually. As such, cooperation among humans can be understood as joint behavior between two or more individuals that is organized along mutually acknowledged principles in order to achieve mutually accepted goals. This describes a wide range of activities, from mundane and short-term endeavors such as two children building a sandcastle at the beach together to grand endeavors like writing a constitution, a task that usually involves dozens of individuals and affects millions more.

Ultimately, any theory of cooperation must address two issues. The first relates to how cooperative ventures are formed in the first place and the second to how cooperative structures are maintained once they are formed. If it is true that individual self-interested rationality is a powerful, ever-present motivator that steers individuals away from cooperative social formations, then a plausible story must be given as to why other phenomena can serve as equally strong motivators that work in the opposite direction, that is, toward cooperation.

One overlooked fact is that, at times, the primary impediments to cooperation are the constraints that bounded rationality imposes on human decision-making. As already noted, human rationality is marked by limited information-processing capacity and additionally is bound by time constraints that limit agents' ability to form and execute optimal decisions. It is unlikely that an individual can either remember or discover all the possible optimal or near-optimal combinations of choices that he has at his disposal in a given instance. The boundedly rational nature of humans implies that the course of action that individuals undertake will inevitably be executed with some degree of inefficiency. Individuals are thus constrained to satisfy a minimum requirement or to do the best they can under a given set of constraints. So, even if the best course of action is to cooperate, it is not always possible to understand that given the cognitive and temporal constraints we face.

Of course, bounded rationality only represents one aspect of the constraints that agents face. Indeed, human beings are bounded in a multitude of ways, and every day we confront situations that force us to behave within cognitive, legal, and moral bounds, even though we may prefer not to. Moreover, for much of our lives, we are dependent on others to accomplish tasks that we cannot accomplish alone. In other words, we are forced to cooperate, and it does not take long to come upon the broadly Hobbesian idea that the reason human beings form stable cooperative relationships in the first place is because they have to out of necessity. Cooperation can thus be viewed largely as an adaptation that individuals develop because of environmental challenges that they cannot overcome alone. We discuss this point further in Chapter 3.

In a well-known game theoretic study of cooperation, Axelrod and Hamilton (1981) identified three requirements for the possible emergence of cooperative behavior. First, it is essential that individuals be involved in an ongoing relationship. If individuals encounter each other only once or very sporadically, they will probably not be inclined to cooperate. This fact indicates that our view of cooperation as a rational or irrational action might change over time. As individuals continuously interact and begin to trust each other, defection could turn out to be an irrational strategy given the objective benefits of cooperation. The second requirement is that individuals must be able to identify each other. The third and final requirement is that individuals must have information about how others have behaved in the past. If another's identity is unknown or unstable or if there is no memory of past interactions, individuals will be motivated to behave selfishly because they will not be accountable for their actions. If we are able to determine whether someone is inclined to cooperate based on past interactions, then it is in our own interest to trust this person and to reciprocate trust to improve our own reputation as a cooperator. Establishing a reputation requires repetition due to the simple fact that a reputation can only be established over time.

The repetition argument gives a simple explanation of why people trust each other and why they reciprocate trust. In many interactions, trust and reciprocity provide the possibility of receiving high payoffs for individuals. In these instances, individuals will hesitate to exploit each other, because the exploited individual might break off the beneficial relationship. Given that most social interaction is not anonymous, it is plausible that, over time, we learn about various decision strategies that are best adapted to different social environments. If a novel situation is encountered, we will likely use a strategy that was applied to a past situation most like the current one we find ourselves in.

1.5 Social Norms, Social Roles, and Reciprocity

Social norms form the bedrock of reciprocity in human societies. For human beings, norms set boundaries on the actions that individuals can carry out. While norms can be characterized as distinct motivators of action just as desires are, they have traditionally been viewed as inhibitors of action, as they demarcate the praxeological terrain that individuals are restricted to.

Humans no doubt refrain from executing many actions because they conflict with the normative prescriptions and proscriptions that an individual has agreed to abide by, either implicitly or explicitly, by being a member of a particular community or social group. Of course, two individuals who are subject to a given norm might be constrained by it in varying degrees. One individual might have more "allegiance" to a norm, believing that it cannot be jettisoned as easily as another individual. Moreover, different individuals may disagree as to when the norm applies even if they have the same level of commitment to it. Their disagreement may be over defeasibility conditions, i.e., over which conditions block the norm from application.

Norms have an important relationship with agents' intentions, which are the primary catalysts of human action. We can of course identify intentions and actions that are not constrained by norms. In this group, we would presumably include the intentions that one forms every day to eat, go to the bathroom, and other biologically induced intentions. The motivation to form such intentions is connected to the organismic drives that individuals have. However, even in the case of biologically induced intentions, norms still play a regulatory role. Consider, for example, someone who forms an intention to eat something. Invariably, what they eat will be constrained by the culture they have been socialized in. In the United States, for example, it is unlikely that the intention to eat something will be filled in by an intention to eat another person. The carrying out of such an intention will undoubtedly be sanctioned by the society in which an agent finds himself.

With the foregoing in mind, we can state without much controversy that in general, biologically induced intentions cannot be considered rational or irrational, but rather *non-rational*, because they are not supported by reasons. For the person who says "I plan to eat something," it seems incorrect to say to that person that he is being rational or irrational. But the same person who says "I plan to eat another person" would probably be considered psychotic or deviant, hence irrational. This person would not be considered deviant, however, if they uttered the same sentence in a society where cannibalism is accepted. They would be considered completely rational and levelheaded. Thus, it seems, for actions and attitudes to be considered rational, some criteria are necessary. Criteria in turn are provided by a social context. The latter notion has been explored in detail by Cass Sunstein (1996). Sunstein argued that it is difficult to conceive of a notion of rationality divorced from social attitudes of approval and disapproval because any idea of rationality divorced from a social context would be unintelligible. Rather, Sunstein argued, social attitudes, what he called "social norms," are the sole determinants of what actions and attitudes are rational, even those typically taken to be in the province of individual rationality. Thus, Sunstein turned the notion of rationality on its head by characterizing individual rationality as not separate or opposed to collective rationality but dependent on it.

To see what Sunstein had in mind, consider an example of his concerning an anti-littering norm. If such a norm is adopted, it is presumably because a community of individuals has deemed it in their self-interest to refrain from littering. And they have probably deemed it in their self-interest to refrain from littering because other social norms have led them to this conclusion. Thus, Sunstein concluded, even actions that we call "self-interested actions" are always a function of social norms. We can think of other examples, such as the accumulation of wealth. Capitalism, which sanctions the pursuit of money as an acceptable endeavor, could be considered the social motivator of the desire to accumulate money beyond what one needs for a comfortable life. Although any individual must accumulate resources to some extent in order to survive, the vigor with which they are accumulated, and the priority their accumulation is given, differs from one society to the next. Of course, social norms also often go against individuals' self-interest and require them to make substantive sacrifices. Nevertheless, we may conclude that social norms are not only regulators of self-interested behaviors but also often their source.

It makes sense to stop at this point and examine what the path is from biological desires to norms. That is, how and why do individuals begin engaging in processes that lead to the establishment of norms that often control and at times even override their biological drives? As noted, humans often need each other to accomplish certain tasks. But once the need for cooperation is acknowledged, the practical need to solve coordination problems with others emerges. In light of this, the establishment of norms can be seen as one way of solving coordination problems. Again, since humans are boundedly rational individuals, and since there is a limit to the knowledge that they possess, it is likely that norms emerge in part when the complexity of a decision surpasses the deliberative capacities of individuals. Moreover, in recurrent situations, it is costly to make the same, even simple, decisions time after time. Thus, individuals utilize norms and rules of thumb as devices to efficiently facilitate basic action (de Waal, 2003).

Within the broader social context of a community, however, there are *social roles*, which are sets of social norms that must be adhered to by any individual conforming to that role. Social roles have a part to play in deciding what the appropriate social norm to follow is in a given instance. For example, suppose a building is on fire. The firefighters present at the scene are working furiously to put out the flames on the eastern side of the blaze, and as they are doing so, a civilian driving by decides to help. Without saying anything, the civilian gets out of his car and begins to put out flames on the western side of the blaze with a fire extinguisher he had stashed away in his car. Now, the civilian is not a firefighter, and thus has not committed to and is not expected to conform to that role. If the civilian had continued to drive by, he would not have been sanctioned in any way. Alternatively, we can imagine a variation of the same scenario where one of the firefighters suddenly dropped his hose, said "I'm through!" and walked away. In this case, the firefighter would be sanctioned, by the city, his colleagues, the general public, and so on. This is because there are certain expectations that go along with the social role of being a firefighter. These expectations set the criteria for what counts as rational or irrational behavior on the part of the person filling that role. If a firefighter suddenly drops his hose and walks away, most would deem that as an instance of irrational behavior. Conversely, if a civilian refrained from helping in putting out the fire, he would not be considered irrational. His actions might even be considered highly rational, given the danger he would expose himself and others to by getting involved, given his lack of expertise in firefighting.

It is noteworthy that non-human animals, especially primates, also have clearly defined social roles within their societies. Dominance hierarchies and parental relationships are the most common, but finer-grained roles like "ally" are also present. Moreover, research has shown that not only do primates occupy and organize their behavior according to social roles but that they are actually aware of their role as well as the roles of others in their group (Seyfarth and Cheney, 2003). It is possible to use the concepts of personal identity and social role interchangeably in the sense that personal identity can be understood to be a matter of the various ways in which individuals might identify with different social roles.

Some accounts of personal identity assume that individuals choose identities that deliver social status and utility within specific groups (Akerlof, 1980). The "theory of conformity" presented by Bernheim is in line with this idea (Bernheim, 1994). According to Bernheim, individuals in groups are concerned with the reactions of other group members. Their concern leads them to respect norms whose observance provides them status in those groups. If individuals have a strong preference for status in a given group, they will be willing to conform to group norms because they recognize that even small deviations from those norms will seriously impair their acceptance in the group. In effect, by moving beyond only a concern with reputation, which is centered on the individual, to a concern with conformity, which centers on the group, an attempt is made to explain how the drive to maximize individual utility can promote social cohesion.

Bernheim distinguished between *individualists* and *conformists*. Individualists are those individuals who have "extreme preferences" in the sense that they are non-conformists who do not abide by social norms. Most individuals, however, are motivated by a desire for conformity that leads them to suppress their individuality to some extent. Further, if individuals have multiple social identities, they could be said to have multiple utility functions that are invoked at different times.

The foregoing discussion points to the most important feature of a social environment in terms of learning and following norms: the reactions of other people. A person's behavior alone is not enough to differentiate correct from incorrect adherence to norms, which are inherently public acts. Rather, it is affirmative or negative social reactions that determine the criteria for what constitutes conformance to a norm. Standards of correctness for norms are possible only if there can be external evaluations of correct or incorrect behavior. An agreement among individuals, akin to what Wittgenstein (1958) called "agreement in judgment," is necessary to establish social norms. This is an agreement in what people do and how they react to each other's behavior in different situations. This agreement is not agreement in opinions or beliefs, the type that commonly results as the product of discourse between people. Rather, it is the normative coordination that obtains within a group of people that allows them to behave in certain uniform ways and to react to other people's behavior in certain uniform ways. The agreement does not have to be a conscious agreement and it is often not. The people in a group might simply take certain modes of conduct for granted. But whether it is conscious or not, such an agreement regulates human affairs. Such a position was also echoed by Rawls (2001):

> Social cooperation is distinct from merely socially coordinated activity — for example, activity coordinated by orders issued by an absolute central authority. Rather, social cooperation is guided by publicly recognized rules and procedures that those cooperating accept as appropriate to regulate their conduct.

Rawls also believed that true cooperation must be regulated by rules that are known and accepted, whether explicitly or implicitly, by those individuals that are a party to a given instance of cooperation. As Rawls pointed out, if a society was organized solely by decrees handed down from the government, it could not be said that the society was composed of cooperating individuals. Although the individuals in such a society would be subject to rules, they would not be aware of the rationale for following them nor would they have the opportunity to modify them or protest against them.

According to Rawls, a general feature of all rules is that they promote the ordering of individuals' actions. This attribute seems to hold for both informal and spontaneously emerging norms and conventions and more formally codified and rationally calculated laws. Rules spell out (to various degrees) what actions individuals must, can, or cannot carry out when engaged in a given instance of collective action. This regulatory feature of rules aids individuals in forming mutual expectations, which are needed in order to make explicit the division of labor among individuals. Clearly defining the role of each participant in a cooperative act prevents unnecessary overlap in duties and also forces individuals to take responsibility for specific duties. Cooperation involves more than mere coordination because it requires a conscious commitment on the part of the individuals doing the cooperating to abide by established precepts. The idea of commitment is important because, among other things, it allows individuals to be sanctioned if they deviate from socially acceptable behavior.

It is important to note that, strictly speaking, we do not need rules in the sense that Rawls spoke of them as public and commonly acknowledged, to order ourselves psychologically. Nevertheless, a great deal of our behavior is ordered by such rules because much of our action is collective action that is either done in concert with others in pursuit of cooperative goals or has an impact on the actions and well-being of others. Thus, there is a need to codify patterns of behavior so that cooperating individuals can form expectations and act accordingly. The need for the codification of patterns is especially important in the realm of geopolitical interaction, which we discuss next.

1.6 Rational Agency in International Affairs

Now that we have provided an overview of the various theories of rationality and cooperation that have informed thinking in social science and philosophy, in this section, we describe the major concepts and theories of international relations that utilize many of the ideas discussed previously. Investors of course need to take an investment-process-specific approach to geopolitical analysis. Unlike their counterparts in government or academia, investors need to determine what geopolitical developments are relevant or irrelevant to their portfolios. Given this, here we define *geopolitical risk* in a portfolio management context as "any potential detriment to a portfolio's positions stemming from political and political-economic actions within and among states and/or non-state actors." Our starting point is to define our *units of analysis* by adapting a well-known framework provided by Waltz (1959). The framework was originally developed to describe interstate conflict and formalizes three levels of analysis: individual, state, and interstate.[1] Here, we adopt Waltz's tripartite structure but modify it so that we can use it as a tool to explain the potential sources of geopolitical risk as they pertain to investment portfolios. Before describing the framework in detail, we note that the different levels of analysis are not necessarily mutually exclusive. Indeed, in most cases, each level of analysis will inform portfolio management to a differing degree. As such, assessments of geopolitical risk will generally be made in an all-things-considered manner. Before developing an overarching framework for conducting geopolitical analysis, it is important to construct what we call a *worldview*.[2] Developing a worldview entails developing a specific theoretical orientation that guides one's research. A worldview includes assumptions about what the primary goals of international actors are and the fundamental nature of the international system. It is roughly analogous to the "mental models" that most investors have regarding the primary drivers of markets. Developing a worldview is a major preoccupation of theorizing in academic international relations research and one whose embrace by investors conducting geopolitical analysis would, we believe, bring welcome clarity to their ideas.

The major schools of international relations theory provide worldviews that stand in stark contrast to one another. For example, *Realism* contends that international relations are primarily a struggle for power between states (the primary unit of analysis) who are

---

[1]Waltz also referred to these levels of analysis as *images*. Waltz used the term *international system* for the third level of analysis. Our labeling reflects its somewhat different characterization in our framework compared to Waltz's.

[2]Here, we are directly inspired by the German concept of *Weltanschauung*.

attempting to survive in an anarchic world. Realism can be further divided into *Defensive Realism*, which views states as being primarily concerned with their own security (they are "security maximizers"), and *Offensive Realism*, which views states as being primarily concerned with the attainment of power, with the ultimate goal of becoming regional hegemons.[3] Realism, especially Offensive Realism, assumes that states are primarily concerned with the attainment of gains relative to other states rather than absolute improvement in their well-being. Thus, states are assumed to view international relations as a zero-sum game. This assumption stands in contrast to the school of international relations known as *Liberalism*, which assumes that states recognize that they are interdependent in a multitude of ways and, as a result, generally seek to build institutions and relationships that foster the development of jointly beneficial outcomes. Further, in Liberalism, states are assumed to be more concerned with absolute gains rather than their standing relative to other states.[4]

With the foregoing in mind, we examine our first level of analysis: *individuals*. This category typically encompasses state and military leaders, but could presumably include non-state individuals such as the Secretary-General of the United Nations and the heads of large terrorist groups. As in the case of international conflict, individual leaders can also pose unique risks to investors. For example, assume that a given country has an economic and market system that possesses features that are deemed desirable by certain investors. It may nevertheless be the case that a particular leader exhibits behaviors and views that override, at least for the period that he/she is in office, the otherwise attractive features of that country's investment climate. For a specific example, consider the case of Turkey. The country has several significant and deep-rooted structural problems, which have been compounded since 2003 when Recep Tayyip Erdoğan began to rule the country. Erdoğan has arguably served to undermine much of the (admittedly modest) institutional

---

[3] Waltz's framework (1979) is widely considered the canonical statement of defensive realism. Mearsheimer (2001) provided the original outline and argument for offensive realism.

[4] The classic statement of the neoliberal view was provided by Keohane (1984).

progress Turkey had made over the two decades preceding his tenure. The institutional erosion precipitated by Erdoğan's rule extends from the judiciary to monetary policy. For emerging market investors, it could be convincingly argued that as long as Turkey is governed by the precepts of "Erdoğanism," exposure to the Turkish market should be given a strategic underweight relative to a given benchmark or zeroed out altogether.

States, our second level of analysis, are defined as the aggregation of institutions which regulate the domestic workings of a given country. There is important interaction between the individual and state levels, as an effective (ineffective) national leader may lessen (increase) the geopolitical risk associated with the structure of a state's underlying institutions. State leaders have varying skills and abilities. However, as capable as an individual leader is, his/her ultimate effectiveness will almost necessarily be constrained by the institutions present in his/her country's political, fiscal, and monetary order.

State-level risks are often characteristic of emerging markets. This is understandable given that the judicial systems of many emerging markets are not yet fully matured and often dispense justice in an unreliable and arbitrary manner. Moreover, the mechanisms of democracy, such as elections and separation of powers, are often ill-formed in developing countries. As a result, the organizational structure of developing countries is generally more fragile and prone to failure when compared to their developed market counterparts. Nevertheless, although institutional fragility is an important part of assessing the risk associated with emerging markets, it is notoriously difficult to quantify. A common approach to quantifying state-level risk is the production of scores for individual countries. Scores are generally aggregations of values assigned to a country in various categories (e.g., corruption, legal system, and regulatory regime). The scores for each category can be thought of as being roughly analogous to credit ratings that are assigned to corporate bonds.

The third and final level of analysis, *interstate relations*, encompasses the political, military, and economic relations between states. This level of analysis is perhaps the most prominent in the minds of investors when they think of geopolitical risk, as political, economic, and military developments between states often have readily observable market consequences. Indeed, even when countries are blessed with skilled leadership and an effective domestic intuitional structure, they may be plagued by interstate conflicts that hamper economic performance. To appreciate the importance of interstate relations on markets, one need only look at the market gyrations caused by the "trade war" between China and the US during the Trump administration. Another stark example is the damage caused to the Russian market in the aftermath of the sanctions regime initiated against that country by the US and EU beginning in March 2014 as retaliation for the annexation of Crimea and the Russian-backed unrest in Eastern Ukraine. Indeed, the Russian market did not recover its July 2013 level until January 2018.[5]

We highlight two further points related to the relationship between interstate relations and financial markets. First, we should remember that different points of conflict can be more or less global in their impact, both in their geographic reach and their potential to move various markets. For example, US/China interactions almost always have global implications, whereas other interstate interactions often have more localized impacts. A case in point is the political-military tension in the Middle East. When hostilities break out, they are often headline-grabbing, but do not generally put pressure on global markets, save for the oil markets. Of course, these conflicts have the potential (and have come close) to devolving into "World War III" scenarios, but that is a lower probability potentiality. A second point that needs to be kept in mind by any investment professional doing geopolitical analysis is that it is important to understand not only the "hot" sources of potential tension around the globe but also the "frozen" conflicts that may reignite at any moment. The dispute over the Kashmir region between India and Pakistan is a case in point, as is the border tension between China and India.[6] The

---

[5]It goes without saying that any assessment of interstate risk must be multifaceted. Consider again the relations between the US and China. They involve trade relations, intellectual property, the status of Taiwan, and human rights in Hong Kong and within China (e.g., in Xinjiang province). All of these points of conflict have been and will continue to hold the potential to negatively impact the global economy and by extension global markets.

[6]We note that the China–India conflict, while occasionally flaring up into violence, is generally underappreciated as a source of genuine geopolitical risk, at least by investors.

need to keep track of geopolitical risks of varying levels of intensity requires investment firms to maintain both a thorough process for geopolitical analysis and personnel with the requisite competence in the multitude of political-economic systems, cultures, and national histories that drive geopolitics. This is not easy and is arguably one of the reasons why high-quality geopolitical analysis is usually not produced by investment firms.

Determining the relevant unit of analysis is but one dimension of analyzing geopolitical risk. A second fundamental aspect of understanding the behavior of global actors is determining whether the primary drivers of their actions are internal or external to them. This distinction is seen most clearly when analyzing state actions. As an example, consider trade policy, which plainly impacts the economic relations between states. In the event of competitive pressures, a government may enact tariffs and/or other trade barriers to protect domestic industries. In this case, the driver of the state's trade policy is external to the country. In other instances, we may imagine situations where there is no exogenous driver of a change in trade policy, but rather it is a state's internal actors who seek to induce a particular change in a state's trade relations. It could be companies belonging to a certain industry who are lobbying the government to reduce tariffs or other trade barriers in order to make the inputs to their industries cheaper or free trade groups who believe in the benefits of maximally liberalized markets.[7]

The interplay between internal and external drivers of geopolitical risk is constant and extends to virtually every policy area. In the zone of security policy, for example, there is the familiar case of a nation's security posture being influenced by the struggle between "hawks" who advocate for a harder military line against a nation's adversaries and "doves" who believe in a softer, more conciliatory approach when dealing with a nation's security challenges. This dynamic is an internal driver of security policy. In contrast, an increase in either aggressive or pacific behavior on the part of a state's adversaries is a potential external driver of a change in security policy. Finally, we

---

[7]For an extended discussion of the tug of war between domestic actors in the realm of exchange rate policy, see Frieden (2015).

note that the jockeying for influence among internal actors is generally only present in states with some semblance of a democratic system, however minimal. In totalitarian systems (e.g., Azerbaijan, North Korea, or Turkmenistan), domestic interest groups, aside from small groups of elites, generally have little to no influence on policymaking.

1.7 Concluding Points

Strictly speaking, the formal modeling of geopolitical interaction does not require a deep understanding of human rationality, the sources of cooperation, or theories of international relations. However, as the world has gotten more politically and economically complex over the years, so have the determinants of global events. Therefore, building realistic models of conflict and cooperation today does require a more nuanced understanding of the varied motivators of human action. This chapter has provided an overview of some of the major concepts and frameworks that have been developed by contemporary researchers in rational choice and international relations. Now that we have described the theoretical foundations of strategic interaction, in the next chapter, we proceed to describe the formal theory of games as it is applied to conflict between agents and show how to simulate various game types using reinforcement learning.

References

Akerlof, G. 1980. A theory of social custom, of which unemployment may be one consequence. *The Quarterly Journal of Economics* 94(4): 749–775

Axelrod, R. and Hamilton, W.D. 1981. The evolution of cooperation. *Science* 211(4489): 1390–1396.

Bernheim, B.D. 1994. A theory of conformity. *Journal of Political Economy* 102(5): 841–877.

de Waal, F.B.M. 2003. Social syntax: The if-then structure of social problem solving. In de Waal F.B.M. and Tyack P.L. (eds.), *Animal Social Complexity: Intelligence, Culture, and Individualized Societies*. Cambridge, MA: Harvard University Press.

Frieden, J.A. 2015. *Currency Politics: The Political Economy of Exchange Rate Policy*. Princeton, NJ: Princeton University Press.

Gauthier, D. 1986. *Morals by Agreement.* Oxford: Clarendon Press.
Keohane, R.O. 1984. *After Hegemony: Cooperation and Discord in the World Political Economy.* Princeton, NJ: Princeton University Press.
Mearsheimer, J.J. 2001. *The Tragedy of Great Power Politics.* New York: Norton.
Sen, A. 1977. Rational fools: A critique of the behavioral foundations of economic theory. *Philosophy and Public Affairs* 6: 317–344.
Sen, A. 1985. Goals, commitment, and identity. *Journal of Law, Economics, and Organization* 1, 341–355.
Sen, A. 2002. *Rationality and Freedom.* Cambridge: Cambridge University Press.
Seyfarth, R.M. and Cheney, D. 2003. Hierarchical social knowledge of monkeys. In de Waal F.B. M. and Tyack P.L. (eds.), *Animal Social Complexity: Intelligence, Culture, and Individualized Societies.* Cambridge, MA: Harvard University Press.
Simon, H. 1957. *Models of Man; Social and Rational.* New York: John Wiley and Sons, Inc.
Sunstein, C. R. 1996. Social norms and social roles. *Columbia Law Review* 96, 903–968.
Waltz, K.N. 1959. *Man, the State, and War: A Theoretical Analysis.* New York: Columbia University Press.
Waltz, K.N. 1979. *Theory of International Politics.* New York: McGraw Hill.
Wittgenstein, L. 1958. *Philosophical Investigations*, Third edition. Translated by Anscombe, G.E.M. Englewood Cliffs: NJ, Prentice Hall.

Chapter 2

Conflict

2.1 Introduction

Although there are various approaches to building models of geopolitical risk, some are more likely than others to provide investors with actionable output. Game theory is perhaps the most commonly used mathematical framework in geopolitical analysis. Indeed, the analytical machinery provided by contemporary game theory provides a practical yet rigorous approach to analyzing strategic interaction among geopolitical actors.[1] In this chapter, we will introduce the formal foundations of game theory and demonstrate how it can be combined with reinforcement learning to simulate conflict between agents over time.

2.2 Agent Preferences

Any analysis of the strategic interaction among agents invariably begins with a characterization of agent preferences. However, the characterization of preferences in geopolitical analyses typically differs from instances of strategic analysis of a more purely economic nature.[2] In economics and finance, assuming that individuals

---

[1]See Osborne and Rubinstein (1994) for a comprehensive mathematical introduction to game theory.

[2]Frieden (1999) provided an extensive discussion of preferences in the context of international relations.

uniformly seek to maximize wealth and that firms universally seek to maximize profit is relatively uncontroversial. In geopolitical analysis, however, we are effectively blocked from assuming uniform preferences across agents, whether they be individuals, states, or non-state actors. States, for example, will have preferences regarding economic and trade issues, security arrangements, human rights, environmental issues, and cultural questions, among others. The multiplicity of preferences in international relations is an especially important factor for investors when they consider the impact of geopolitical developments on financial markets. This is so because non-economic preferences may very well dominate economic preferences among political decision-makers, even though their ultimate decisions will almost certainly impact their countries' economies and markets.

During strategic deliberation, agent preferences interact with the fundamental features of human rationality which we described in the previous chapter: (1) *Boundedness*, which constrains agents' ability to maximally realize their goals. This boundedness not only encompasses agents' computational limitations but also the cognitive biases that may detrimentally impact their decision-making. (2) Both *Synchronic* (short-term) and *diachronic* (long-term) dimensions, the latter which motivates agents to at times eschew present gains for future ones. (3) Its often *non-instrumental* nature, in the sense that individuals' commitments, as opposed to their desires, can serve as the prime motivators of action. We assume that agents in the geopolitical realm are rational in a way that is consistent with this refined picture of human rationality.

By assuming the foregoing characterization of human rationality and decision-making, it is possible to apply game theory to realistically model both cooperative and noncooperative interaction in a variety of contexts and cases. In this chapter, where we focus on noncooperative games, players are in competition or conflict with one another, attempting to secure higher payoffs at the expense of the other player(s) in the game.

2.3 Game Theory Basics

In game theory, a *game* is considered any situation where the outcome for each person depends not only on his or her own action but also on the actions of the people they interact with. Thus, a game consists of two or more *players* engaged in cooperative or competitive action(s) with one another. Two fundamental game theoretic concepts are *Pareto optimality* and *Nash equilibrium*.[3] A game outcome is Pareto optimal if no other outcome is available that makes one individual better off without making another worse off. A game outcome is in Nash equilibrium when each player's action is the best response to the actions of the other players.

In addition to players, games consist of rules and actions. Player actions may be deliberate or random, determined by a roll of the dice, for example. A game can be represented by a matrix with $m \times n$ cells where m and n are the number of moves that each player has. Cells of the matrix contain values, one for each player, which represent the payoffs that the players would receive from their moves given the moves of the other players. The values of the payoffs are decided by the rules of the game and each player tries to choose in a way that leads to the highest payoff possible. Game theory is useful precisely because it explicitly lays out the choices of the players as well as the payoffs that result from the combination of choices made by them. An important result in game theory is that for a number of games, it is always possible to find an equilibrium from which no player should deviate, i.e., there is no move they can make that will lead to a higher payoff for them. These equilibria exist for every two-player game that (1) has a finite number of moves after which the game ends, (2) is a "zero-sum" game, where one player's losses equal their opponent's gain, and (3) has players who know their own moves and preferences as well as those of the other player(s).

2.4 The Prisoner's Dilemma

One of the most frequently studied noncooperative games in game theory is the Prisoner's Dilemma (PD). The PD elegantly illustrates how the expectations of another player's actions can drive specific game outcomes. A commonly articulated description of the PD tells the tale of two criminals who have been apprehended after

---

[3]Pareto (1902) and Nash (1951).

committing a serious crime together. The police do not have evidence to prove that the two committed this crime, but do have evidence to prove that they are guilty of a lesser infraction. The police offer each of the criminals a deal where if they confess to the crime and implicate their partner, they will be exonerated and have the minor charges dropped. In turn, the other prisoner will be incarcerated for a long time. However, the police will only honor the deal if the other prisoner does not confess to the crime. If both prisoners confess, they will each receive a moderate jail term. If neither prisoner confesses, then both of them will be charged with the minor infraction and will be given lighter sentences. The acts of confessing or not confessing are known respectively as "defection" and "cooperation."

In any given instance of the PD, one of the following outcomes will materialize: (1) Both prisoners will defect and each will spend a moderate amount of time in jail, (2) the prisoners will cooperate and each will spend a small amount of time in jail, or (3) one prisoner will defect while the other cooperates, leading to the defector being freed and the cooperator serving a long jail sentence. Without any additional knowledge, the prisoners will behave in a rational manner and will choose the outcome that leads to the highest payoff for each of them: defection. Thus, the game generally results in payoffs to each player that are suboptimal to those they would have received by cooperating.

The PD is useful because it formally presents a major paradox of rationality, that is, how a thoroughly rational action may not always be the best action to take from the standpoint of self-interest. Basic, single-stage PDs generally possess two distinct characteristics that can be easily observed in Table 2.1. The two characteristics are (1) defection as the dominating strategy for each player, i.e., defection is the best strategy no matter how a player's opponent plays, and (2) mutual defection is the only strategy that is not Pareto

Table 2.1. Prisoner's Dilemma.

		Player 2 Cooperate	Player 2 Defect
Player 1	Cooperate	1, 1	0, 10
	Defect	10, 0	5, 5

optimal. From this, it follows that in the case of a one-stage PD, rational agents will defect because defection is the dominating strategy. So, regardless of the other player's strategy, defection maximizes an individual's expected utility. However, since the equilibrium outcome that results from both individuals defecting is Pareto inferior to the non-equilibrium outcome of cooperation, the game leads to a collectively unsatisfactory conclusion. In other words, the individually dominant option and the cooperative option conflict.

The first thing to note is that the usual unsatisfactory outcome of the PD is to an extent due to the fact that the game is "one shot" — conducted in one round of play. Consequently, one of the ways of making the game more conducive to cooperation is to iterate the game over multiple rounds. Through repeated encounters where players learn about each other's propensity to act in certain ways, there is presumably a greater chance for cooperation. That said, we note that it has been shown that in any repeated PD game, there are an infinite number of outcomes that are sustainable as long-run equilibria by rational, self-interested individuals. These outcomes run the gamut from mutually cooperative to mutually noncooperative (Morrow, 1994).

In analyzing multi-stage PD games, Robert Axelrod (1984) demonstrated in a computer tournament that the so-called "tit-for-tat" strategy, where players cooperate in the first round and in subsequent rounds mimic the action of the other player in the previous round, was the best strategy for an individual to follow. It was observed that if tit for tat was followed by both players, the game will produce a Pareto optimal outcome.[4] Axelrod's primary argument for why this is the case is that the precondition for the evolution of cooperation is that players have a sufficiently large chance for future interaction in order for a commitment to reciprocity to evolve. Filling out this idea, Axelrod considered the following as characterizing the basis of cooperation:

(1) Cooperation can develop even in a world comprising only self-interested individuals. It can evolve from small groups of individuals who base their cooperation on reciprocity. However,

---

[4]See Trivers (1971) for much of the research that informs Axelrod's experiments.

cooperation cannot develop if reciprocity is practiced only by dispersed individuals who will not meet in the future.
(2) A strategy based on reciprocity can thrive in a world of diverse strategies.
(3) Cooperation, once established on the basis of reciprocity, can protect itself from invasion by less cooperative strategies.[5]

Thus, according to Axelrod, when players recognize that they have common interests and that there is a high probability of future interaction, cooperation is more likely to occur. This requires that *future payoffs* have to be considered by players so that they see the benefits of their cooperation in the long run. Consideration of future payoffs in turn requires that individuals possess the ability to form expectations about future encounters.[6] Axelrod's solution to the PD is an "internal" one in the sense that players learn to cooperate by building trust. There has, however, been considerable research on "external" solutions to the PD, where cooperation is induced by means of new rules or other introduced game elements. In the following section, we will discuss the structure of external solutions and compare them to internal solutions as we have defined them.

2.4.1 *External and Internal Solutions to the Prisoner's Dilemma*

One way to modify the PD is to change the "rules of the game," where people's attitudes are changed through incentivization or coercion. These external solutions can either be centralized or decentralized depending on the extent to which these attitudinal changes are shared among the members of a group. External solutions, however, seem to operate under the assumption that solutions to other more

---

[5]This has also been shown by Eshel *et al.* (2000) who demonstrated that in a population with a local interaction structure, where individuals interact with their neighbors and learning is done by imitating a successful neighbor, cooperation is a stable strategy that cannot be easily eliminated from a population by a rival strategy. As such, cooperation is what is known as an Evolutionarily Stable Strategy (ESS) (Maynard Smith, 1982).

[6]The ability to form expectations is important for forming intentions and is an ability that humans arguably possess in greater capacity than other animals. This undoubtedly aids humans in forming robust cooperative structures.

elementary collective action problems, like voting or the creation of systems of punishment and reward, have been provided. Therefore, some consider these solutions as second-order elements of collective action because they see the provision of a new set of rules as tantamount to providing another public good (Ostrom, 1990).

In multi-person PDs, a solution is centralized if it is concentrated in the hands of only a few members of the group, as in the case of "the state." As is well known, Hobbes's *Leviathan* (2008) contains the first detailed argument in defense of the existence of the state. He argues that without the coercive power of the state, people could not successfully cooperate and realize their common interest and thus could not provide themselves with certain public goods, especially social order, peace, and security. They would remain in the "state of nature" where life is a brutal struggle of all against all. Since then, many have accepted Hobbes's view as the only correct prescription for curing failures in cooperation and public goods provision.

Another solution to the PD is to influence the payoff structure that each member faces. Ullmann-Margalit[7] presented an example of this type of solution. The example she presented involves two "mortar men" in outposts facing an enemy attack. Each of the men must decide between remaining at his post and fighting or escaping. If both stay and fight, they are able to defend against the enemy. If both escape, the enemy will break through and take both of them prisoner. If one stays at his post while the other escapes, the one who remains will be able to defend against the enemy long enough for the other to escape, but will be killed as the enemy will eventually advance. If both mortar men are aware of their situation, defection — escaping while their fellow soldier stays and fights — gives the highest payoff, just as in the PD. If both soldiers escape, the outcome for both is worse than if they both had stayed and fought, again as in the PD. The goal then becomes to change the payoff structure in order to bring about a situation where both mortar men lose the incentive to flee. One solution presented by Ullmann-Margalit (1977) was to lay mines around the mortar men's posts so that any attempt to escape would result in death. This would presumably provide the

---

[7]Ullmann-Margalit (1977, pp. 30–33).

Table 2.2. Mortar Men with Mines.

		Player 2	
		Fight	Desert
Player 1	Fight	1, 1	−2, −2
	Desert	−2, −2	−2, −2

Table 2.3. Mortar Men with Discipline.

		Player 2	
		Fight	Desert
Player 1	Fight	1, 1	−2, (−1, 0)
	Desert	(−1, 0), −2	−1.5, −1.5

motivation to stay and fight. We show the payoff structure for this game in Table 2.2.

Another external solution to the problem of cooperation in the PD is the threat of punishment. For example, Ullmann-Margalit cited discipline as an example of such a regulatory device. The story of the mortar men with discipline is laid out in the following way: The two mortar men belong to a unit where military discipline is severe. This discipline is embodied in a rule that desertion under enemy fire is punishable by execution. In order to be executed, a deserter has to be caught first. Thus, the uncertainty of execution may provide motivation for a mortar man to escape if a battle looks hopeless or if he realizes that his comrade is escaping. The payoff structure for this game is shown in Table 2.3.

If both soldiers remain in their posts, the payoff (1) is the same as in Table 2.2. Staying and fighting when your comrade escapes also provides the same payoff (−2) as in the previous game. To escape when your comrade also escapes gives a payoff of −1.5, which is more desirable than staying behind and getting killed but less desirable than the payoff of getting caught. This payoff can be constructed by combining the undesirability of getting caught and the probability of being executed. To escape when your comrade stays behind gives a payoff of either −1 or 0 depending upon whether a player is caught and executed or not. The foregoing examples describe open-ended situations where individuals are constrained by various sanctions, the probabilities of which are uncertain. It is worth noting, however, that external solutions are not necessarily restricted to the use of sanctions and rewards. Other solutions, changing people's attitudes via persuasion, for example, can also be treated as external.

Aside from external solutions to the PD, there have been various "internal" or spontaneous solutions, which do not presuppose changes in the game. Included here are all those factors that induce members of a group to voluntarily act for the collective good. This implies that cooperation can evolve without any external pressure. In such situations, all involved usually acknowledge that pursuing self-interest at all times cannot function as a basis for voluntary cooperation. Internal solutions are conceptually in harmony with the idea of reciprocity, which we discussed earlier.

Both external and internal solutions to the PD address two common errors that are often made in trying to explain cooperative behavior. The first is one we have already touched on, that there exists one privileged motivation, self-interest, which explains all instances of cooperation. It seems natural to think that motives other than self-interest should be given a place of eminence within game theory and social science in general, as it is a rare person indeed who will claim to be completely regulated by self-interest alone. The second related error is to believe that each instance of cooperation can be explained by only one motivation. Cooperation, however, actually occurs when different motivations reinforce each other (Elster, 1990).

One alternative motive that arguably drives action is altruism — serving the public good to benefit one or more others. The most commonly proposed source of altruism is empathy, consistent with the perceived welfare of another individual. Seen from an evolutionary perspective, altruism toward the members of a group can be associated with aggression against those outside the group. Members of a group perceive their comrades as similar and therefore empathize with them. Nevertheless, how certain individuals make judgments of similarity is unique to them, and individual perceptions of similarity may extend, as well as limit, agents' ability to take the perspective of others and to behave altruistically toward them. We further note that when individuals are members of a collective and their welfare is connected to the welfare of the collective, actions that satisfy their own interests may appear as instances of altruistic behavior. However, such actions should generally be differentiated from actions motivated by genuine altruism, where an individual's goal is in fact to increase the welfare of a group or collective without consideration for his own payoffs.

2.4.2 The Role of Norms in Solving the Prisoner's Dilemma

Social norms are of course important in solving PD problems. Some have argued that norms arise as spontaneous rules that solve PD problems as unintended consequences of self-interested action (Vanberg, 1994). An important characteristic of social norms is that they require actions on behalf of individuals which are socially beneficial but may be in conflict with an individual's immediate interests. Consider the norm of keeping one's promises. An individual's commitment to keeping promises might benefit them in one situation while in others it may turn out to be against their immediate interests.[8] Prioritizing collective welfare over individual welfare marks a point of similarity between conforming to social norms and engaging in acts of altruism. However, adherence to social norms is typically observed by all members of a group while acts of altruism are typically determined and executed individually. Indeed, an important feature of social norms is that members of a collective view the maintenance of norms as desirable from a "structural" standpoint. Thus, an individual will generally prefer a state of affairs where all participants adhere to a social norm to a state where the rule does not exist because the maintenance of the rule fosters the robustness of their respective collective. This implies that individuals perceive the benefits of maintaining social norms as outweighing the costs of maintaining them.

What has been said so far about social norms can be said about moral rules. In fact, a unique characteristic of moral rules is that they contain the PD problem. To behave morally means to abide by a PD rule whose eradication would be harmful to everyone. But are all social norms also moral rules? According to Gauthier (1986), a system of moral rules is made up of principles that guide individuals' behavior to increase cooperation in PD situations. As in the case

---

[8] Again, we see the potential conflict between diachronic and synchronic self-interest.

of norms, when individuals adopt a system of moral rules, they are often willing to jettison their maximizing choices in order to maintain the perceived benefits of cooperation. Thus, a moral person will not defect in a PD situation, even if he can foresee that those he is interacting with will be unable to exact revenge against him at a later time if he did in fact defect.

Ullmann-Margalit (1977) challenged the forgoing definition of moral rules. She referred to an example where two gangsters behave morally toward each other by not confessing, even though it would be in each party's interest to defect. She questions whether the outcome would be enough for "them to be considered moral men?" Ullmann-Margalit was aware that Gauthier's interpretation would give a positive answer to the latter question whereas her own answer would be negative. She thus suggested a further condition for rules to qualify as *moral* rules: An outcome should not involve "disadvantage to anyone extraneous to the PD-structured situation under consideration." Two things are worth noting about this statement. First, it is true that Gauthier's interpretation does not provide a normative judgment about what specific rules ought to be considered moral rules. The two gangsters may act morally toward each other by tricking or otherwise taking advantage of others. If the two gangsters abide by the moral norms of, e.g., the Mafia, and consider the norms of the larger society irrelevant, then we have a situation where the norms of a group and its subgroup conflict. However, both sets of norms must be justified by referring to and expressing the values of their respective members. Consequently, there seems to be no conclusive way to differentiate between PD norms and moral norms.

The second point in Ullmann-Margalit's interpretation of moral rules that needs to be addressed is the principle that moral rules must not cause harm to anyone extraneous to the particular PD the players find themselves in. The problem with this principle is that it might turn out to be difficult to verify the extent of the unintended negative consequences of specific actions. For example, many of the activities that multinational corporations engage in cause harm to people.[9] Most of these activities are motivated by a desire to turn a profit and are not done to cause any deliberate harm. These activities

---

[9]In economics, these unintended negative consequences are called *negative externalities*.

are, under Ullmann-Margalit's interpretation, immoral. But now we must go back to the initial question about whose values are to be used in assessing moral claims and how to go about verifying the extent of the damage caused by unintended actions.

Insofar as social norms are considered exogenous to PD problems, it is not too difficult to show how the problem is solved. If the payoff structure is modified by the observance of moral rules, then cooperation can be stabilized. Social norms are intriguing as solutions to PD problems because of their endogenous nature. A spontaneous norm that solves a PD problem contains the same PD problem in itself. For example, although the rule of promise-keeping solves PD problems by fostering trust among individuals, it is susceptible to being exploited precisely because of its normative role.

Deciphering which norms international actors are governed by is critical in building realistic models for geopolitical analysis. Because the PD game form is so ubiquitous in geopolitical contexts, it is important to understand it, including potential solutions to it, both internal and external. But there are a number of other important games of conflict to consider, as they are also prevalent in international affairs. Before we do so, however, in the next section, we briefly discuss a challenge to a major assumption of game theory relating to how payoffs are perceived by the players in a game.

2.5 Intermezzo: Absolute or Relative Payoffs?

While the standard assumptions of game theory often facilitate informative analyses of real-life strategic situations, they sometimes fail to do so in important ways. For example, one of the problematic assumptions from game theory is that players are only concerned with absolute payoffs. This assumption is at odds with the realities of many types of geopolitical interactions. For example, consider the game shown in Table 2.4. Under the standard assumptions of game theory, the equilibrium solution is Row 1 — Column 1 with a payoff of (10,10). However, a well-known study by Marvell and Schmitt (1968) found that experimental results generally deviate from those implied by the assumptions of game theory. Specifically, they reported that the most common result is that found in Row 2 — Column 1, indicating that players are often willing to sacrifice their absolute gains to

Table 2.4. Maximizing Difference.

		Player 2	
		Column 1	Column 2
Player 1	Row 1	10, 10	3, 2
	Row 2	9, 3	2, 1

a certain extent in order to ensure a significant deterioration in their opponent's position, an objective that is called *maximizing difference*.

It is possible to think of the sacrificed payoff as a cost that one player is willing to pay in order to secure a stronger position relative to another player.[10] For example, country **A** may refuse to sell a certain type of technology to neighboring country **B** in order to prevent the latter from developing its economy, even though **A** will get a lower economic payoff due to it depriving itself of an additional market. The motivation for country **A** could be to maintain regional military dominance in relation to country **B**.

2.6 Games of Conflict Beyond the Prisoner's Dilemma

Aside from the PD, there are a host of games that are used to represent different types of human conflicts. One important type of noncooperative game is what is known as the *Attack–Defense Game*, where one player wishes to change the status quo and another player wants to preserve it. An example of this type of game is the *Run–Pass Game*.[11] The game is usually articulated as a competition between two (American) football teams. One team, *Offense*, is contemplating its next play. That latter team has two options: It can choose to either run or pass. The second team, *Defense*, can choose to either defend against a run or defend against a pass. If *Offense* runs while *Defense* defends against pass, then *Offense* gains a payoff of five

---

[10] See Ulmann-Margalit (1977) for a more detailed discussion of the concept of maximizing difference.
[11] The Run–Pass game is a slightly more sophisticated variant of a well-known game called *Matching Pennies*. For an extensive discussion of Matching Pennies, see Weirich (1998).

Table 2.5. Run–Pass Game 1.

		Defense	
		Defend Pass	Defend Run
Offense	Pass	0, 0	10, −10
	Run	5, −5	0, 0

yards while *Defense* gets a payoff of negative five yards. However, if *Defense* correctly predicts *Offense's* play, then both *Offense* and *Defense* gain a payoff of zero yards. On the other hand, if *Offense* passes and *Defense* defends against a run, then *Offense* gains a payoff of ten yards while *Defense* gets a payoff of negative ten yards. The payoff matrix corresponding to the Run–Pass game is shown in Table 2.5.

There are many types of geopolitical interaction that are analogous to the Run–Pass game. Perhaps the most obvious example is political-military conflict, where warring sides try to deduce and predict each other's respective points of weakness. However, the game may also be applied to non-military engagements such as trade negotiations. For example, one side of a negotiation may be considering which of two possible concessions to ask for in the current round of negotiations. They may surmise that the other party to the negotiation will be more amenable to giving one concession rather than another. This could be the case for a variety of reasons, such as one party's belief that their negotiating partner is under pressure from domestic interest groups (e.g., trade groups or labor unions) to bring negotiations on a specific item to a close.[12] The game can also be used to model monetary policy actions that are driven by the strategic interactions between central banks. Central banks can choose to adjust interest rates, the money supply, or other policy tools in anticipation of or as a response to changes in the economy and actions by other central banks. By modeling this interaction as

---

[12]It might be remarked that the results of a negotiation are typically not zero sum as in the Run–Pass game. However, it is possible to assume that the payoffs denote the amount of *relative* benefit transferred to one party from another as a result of negotiations, analogous to the territory gained or lost in military engagements.

a Run–Pass game, investors can analyze the potential outcomes of different policy choices and identify the optimal strategies for each central bank. For example, we may model how a central bank of an exporting country determines the appropriate level of interest rates in anticipation of a certain policy from the central bank of a rival exporter in a given economic environment. In this case, instead of Run and Pass, we may model the actions Lower Rates and Maintain Rates. We may choose to modify payoffs in various ways as well, but the basic formal architecture of the game will remain the same.

It is important to note that in international affairs, most strategic exchanges occur over an extended period of time and are hence more accurately modeled as multi-period interactions. Thus, from a formal standpoint, international relations are most faithfully modeled using the format of iterated games discussed earlier.[13] In the next section, we introduce one approach to modeling geopolitical interactions in this way.

2.7 Analyzing Games Using Contextual Multi-Armed Bandits

While there are several approaches to modeling iterative games, we have found that the reinforcement learning framework known as the *Contextual Multi-Armed Bandit* (CMAB) allows more sophisticated types of games to be modeled in a manner that is both computationally tractable and transparent.[14] A CMAB is a reinforcement learning algorithm that is often used in situations where a decision-maker needs to repeatedly choose from a set of available options. In reinforcement learning, an algorithm learns the optimal solution to a problem through the rewards and punishments it receives when taking specific actions. In bandit problems, the goal is to maximize

---

[13] Aside from Axelrod (1981), multi-period games are also analyzed in detail in Maynard Smith and Price (1973).
[14] Some view contextual bandits as sitting between standard multi-armed bandits and "genuine" reinforcement learning frameworks. This is due to the fact that although contextual bandits incorporate states, agents' actions do not influence the state as in standard reinforcement learning algorithms. We will discuss these types of algorithms in Chapter 4.

the accumulative payoff or minimize the expected regret over a set of repeated actions.[15] A multi-armed bandit is like a slot machine with more than one arm, with each arm representing an action that an agent can take.

CMABs have some inherent game theoretic characteristics, which also add to their appeal in the present context. Recall that in an iterative game, each player has multiple strategies they can employ, and the optimal strategy will depend on the strategies of the other players over time. In each round, players observe the outcomes of the previous round and adjust their strategies accordingly. This is similar to the problem faced by agents as they are modeled within a CMAB algorithm, where the *exploitation* of options that have performed well in the past must be balanced with the *exploration* of new options. To model an iterative game using a CMAB, each player's available strategies can be considered "arms" on a slot machine. The algorithm uses information from previous rounds to estimate the performance of each arm and then uses a decision rule to select the optimal action (arm) for the current round. Modelers can then observe the dynamic adjustments that players make over time based on feedback and context, leading to insight regarding the ultimate utility of any given strategy over time.

True to their name, CMABs also utilize what are known as *contexts*, which are the states of the world in which the players of the game find themselves. The use of contexts allows us to model what are known as *games of incomplete information*, also known as *Bayesian games*. In the language of Bayesian games, contexts can be characterized as representing a player's *type*, which refers to its character or nature. Types are expressed within individual games by unique sets of payoffs. For example, consider the matrices in Tables 2.6 and 2.7, which represent a game where Player 1 faces an opponent of unknown strength. Player 1's type is known, but Player 2's type is not. Player 2 can be "strong" with probability α or "weak" with probability $1 - \alpha$. As we can see, this game adds a layer of complexity to the players' deliberation process as they must

---

[15]The multi-armed bandit problem was first studied in mathematical detail by Robbins (1952) and Gittins (1979). For further discussion of the multi-armed bandit problem, see Katehakis and Veinott (1987). Contextual bandit problems are also analyzed in Dudik et al. (2011). An overview of reinforcement learning applications to game theory is provided in Crandall and Goodrich (2011).

Table 2.6. Strong Opponent.

		Player 2	
		Fight	Capitulate
Player 1	Fight	−1, 1	1, 0
	Capitulate	0, 1	0, 0

Table 2.7. Weak Opponent.

		Player 2	
		Fight	Capitulate
Player 1	Fight	1, −1	1, 0
	Capitulate	0, 1	0, 0

Table 2.8. Run–Pass Game 2.

		Defense	
		Defend Pass	Defend Run
Offense	Pass	−2, −1	3, −3
	Run	2, −2	−3, −2

consider the states of the world, represented by player types, that they may encounter when playing a particular game.

Any game can be transformed into a Bayesian game. For example, we may use the payoff matrix in Table 2.5 with that in 2.8 to create a Bayesian version of the Run–Pass game.

The game in Table 2.8 has the same structure as the game in Table 2.5. However, the differences between the payoffs resulting from different action combinations in Table 2.8 are narrower than those found in Table 2.5. In fact, if the players find themselves in the context of Table 2.8, *Offense* will be facing a disastrous outcome given that in the event of a successful defense, *Offense* will sustain greater damage than *Defense*. In real-world terms, such a game may correspond to a type of defender that is more prepared and/or better equipped relative to an attacking force. When the possibility of encountering the latter type of defender is present, it must be a consideration that enters into the deliberations of a potential attacker.

However, in a Bayesian game, in order to understand what course of action is beneficial to an attacker, we must also attach probabilities to each context and then observe the probability-weighted average payoffs accruing to each action over time. As noted, CMABs can be used to gain insight into iterated Bayesian games as they give us the ability to formalize the notion of a type as context. Because contexts are vectors of features (probabilities and payoffs) that are assigned to each arm in a CMAB, they naturally lend themselves to the representation of types in simulations of iterated Bayesian games. We examine how to construct such simulations in the next section.

2.8 Simulating Iterated Games Using CMABs

In this section, we show how to build simulations of iterated games using CMABs. In each simulation we present, it is assumed that at each time step t agents are presented with contextual information. Each context has a specific probability of materializing. Once a context is presented to agents, they choose an action a from K possible actions and are presented with a reward r for the action. We then observe the average payoffs over time for each action. The payoff for each action also has a specific probability attached to it. Thus, in the simulations, we are calculating *expected payoffs*, which are the product of a gain (loss) amount and a probability that the gain (loss) obtains. Differences in gain (loss) amounts need not be precisely calibrated amounts but can simply reflect relative differences in the value of perceived action combinations.

Before showing the results of a simulation with the foregoing framework, we describe the particular algorithm that we use to implement it. There are various algorithms that can be used to drive a CMAB. We implement our CMAB using what is known as the Upper Confidence Bound (UCB) algorithm.[16] An important aspect

---

[16] We use the UCB algorithm because it provides a balance between effectiveness and simplicity. It is one of several popular algorithms available for application to multi-armed bandit problems. In Chapter 5, we will consider Thompson sampling, another algorithm that is commonly used in bandit frameworks.

For further reading on the UCB algorithm, see Auer (2002) and Chu *et al.* (2011).

of the UCB is that it attempts to balance *exploitation* versus *exploration*, which we mentioned earlier. With exploitation, we select the optimal choices that we are already familiar with. With exploration, we take some risks and choose an option whose benefits are unknown to us. The difference between the two is akin to choosing to eat at one of your favorite restaurants versus trying a new establishment. We present the formal details of the UCB algorithm in Table 2.9.

We are now in a position to present our simulations, in which we recast the basic Run–Pass game within a CMAB. In each simulation, we model the evolution of payoffs for different actions over a multitude of iterations. An important aspect of our simulations is that we take the point of view of one of the players in the game. We do this to facilitate expository clarity. Thus, while we are objective

Table 2.9. Upper Confidence Bound Algorithm.

For K possible actions, at any time $t > K$

Initialize, for all actions a:

$N_a(t) \leftarrow 0$

$Q_t(a) \leftarrow 0$

Repeat for $t = 1, 2, \ldots,$

$a \leftarrow \mathrm{argmax}_a \left(Q_t(a) + c\sqrt{\frac{\log t}{N_a(t)}} \right)$

$r \leftarrow \mathrm{reward}(a)$

$N_a(t) \leftarrow N_a(t) + 1$

$Q_t(a) \leftarrow Q_t(a) + \frac{1}{N_a(t)} \left(r - Q_t(a) \right)$

where $Q_t(a)$ is the average real-valued payoff to taking action a and $N_a(t)$ is the number of times an action has been taken. The term $\sqrt{\frac{\log t}{N_a(t)}}$ represents the confidence interval for the average reward. The parameter c is a constant that controls the degree of exploration.

observers of the evolution and results of a simulation, we nevertheless evaluate outcomes from one player's point of view. As a rule, we will take the point of view of Player 1. It is of course advisable that researchers analyze outcomes from the standpoint of all the players in a game in order to get a comprehensive picture of strategic dynamics.

Our specific implementation of the CMAB uses the payoff matrices in Tables 2.5 and 2.8 respectively as Strong and Weak types (contexts). First, probabilities are assigned to payoffs for a given type. In our example, we assign a probability of 0.30 that *Offense* is of the Strong Passer type and a probability of 0.70 that *Offense* is of the Weak Passer type. We further assign a 0.60 probability that *Offense* is of the Strong Runner type and a 0.40 probability that *Offense* is of the Weak Runner type. Next, we assign probabilities to *Offense's* chance of success *given* a specific type. By "chance of success," we mean the probability that *Offense* will Run while *Defense* defends Pass. For the action Pass, we posit a success probability of 0.70 if *Offense* is of the Strong Passer type and 0.40 if *Offense* is of the Weak Passer type. For the action Run, we posit a success probability of 0.80 if *Offense* is of the Strong Runner type and 0.30 if *Offense* is of the Weak Runner type. We have six "arms" in our model — one arm to determine the type for Run and one arm to determine the type for Pass, and four to determine the respective probabilities of specific action combinations (e.g., Run/Defend Pass). However, we note that in any given iteration of the game, only four of the six arms are utilized ("pulled"). The first two arms, which determine the types for Run and Pass, are always used. Of the remaining four arms, which ones are activated depends on the types determined for Run and Pass. At the end of our simulation, we observe the evolution of average payoffs for two actions, Run and Pass, over time. For macro investors, the simulations can be used to provide some *ex ante* insight into the actions of political-economic actors, which can then inform their investment processes. We further note that the way we have set up the implementation of the simulations is not the only way to do so. However, we believe that our implementation is relatively transparent and computationally straightforward.

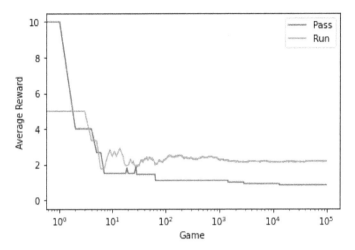

Figure 2.1. Evolution of Payoffs for Run–Pass Game (First Iteration).

In Figure 2.1, we show the evolution of payoffs for each action in our Run–Pass game. We see that Run has a higher average payoff over the entire set of iterations (10^5 games), despite the fact that it has lower positive payoffs compared to Pass in either context — 10 and 3 for Pass vs. 5 and 2 for Run. This result is also interesting because Pass has a higher success probability if it is of the Strong Passer type. Thus, the higher probability of Pass being of the Weaker Passer type outweighs the higher payoff (10) and the higher probability of success attached to a Strong Passer type. That said, Figure 2.1 also shows that in the earlier iterations of the game, it is Pass which exhibits a higher average payoff. And until right before 10^1 iterations, there is an oscillation between the relative size of the average payoffs for Run and Pass, at which point Run begins to establish itself as the action with the higher long-run average payoff.

In any type of simulation, it is generally beneficial to conduct some type of "sensitivity analysis" where key input parameters in a simulation are changed and the model is rerun. The purpose of this exercise is to observe the dependence of simulation outcomes on the precise values of the most important inputs. For example, in the Run–Pass game we are examining, it appears that the probability of *Offense* being a Strong Passer or Weak Passer type is the determining

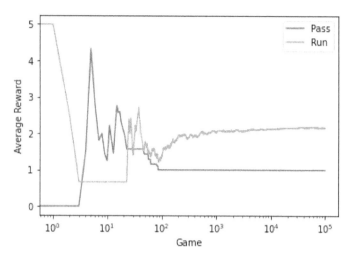

Figure 2.2. Evolution of Payoffs for Run–Pass Game (Second Iteration).

factor in the longer-term payoffs for each action. Let us test this assumption by modifying the probability that *Offense* is a Strong Passer type to 0.40, i.e., increasing its probability of being a Strong Passer type by 0.10. When we do so, we see in Figure 2.2 that there is a marked change in the relative trajectories of average payoffs for each action. Nevertheless, Run once again exhibits a higher long-run average payoff as more and more games are played.

What else do the results in Figures 2.1 and 2.2 tell us? Well, at least in this example, the results tell us that we need to be attentive to the accuracy of our probability assignments. While the positive payoffs assigned to Pass and Run seem to differ significantly, the long-run average payoffs in both simulations are predominately driven by the type probability assigned to Pass. Another takeaway here is that we must be attentive to the number of rounds in the simulation. As we see, the winning strategy can change over time. And since each iteration represents an actual unit of time (e.g., month or year) the length of the simulation must reasonably reflect, to the extent possible, the actual length of a bout of geopolitical interaction. Finally, we see that the structure of the game is relatively stable and sensitive to a rather moderate change in the input parameters. If we proceeded to modify additional input parameter values and continued to see similar results over the life of the simulation, then that would further support our confidence in the robustness of the model.

2.9 Concluding Points

In this chapter, we have provided an overview of the foundations of game theory, reviewed a number of noncooperative games, and demonstrated how to simulate Bayesian games using contextual multi-armed bandit algorithms. As we emphasized in the chapter, in setting up any realistic model of strategic interaction, it is important that thorough consideration be given to the goals, desires, and commitments of the players, as well as the inputs to the model at hand. In the next chapter, we will take the same approach to examine cooperative games and their application to geopolitical analysis.

References

Auer, P. 2002. Using confidence bounds for exploitation-exploration tradeoffs. *Journal of Machine Learning Research* 3(Nov): 397–422.

Axelrod, R. 1981. The evolution of cooperation. *Science* 211(4489): 1390–1396.

Axelrod, R. 1984. *The Evolution of Cooperation.* New York: Basic Books.

Chu, W., Li, L., Reyzin, L., and Schapire. R., Contextual bandits with linear payoff functions. In *Proceedings of the Fourteenth International Conference on Artificial Intelligence and Statistics*, 208–214.

Crandall, J.W. and Goodrich, M.A. 2011. Learning to compete, coordinate, and cooperate in repeated games using Reinforcement Learning. *Machine Learning* 82(3): 281–314.

Dudik, M., Hsu, D., Kale, S., Karampatziakis, N., Langford, J., Reyzin, L. and Zhang, T. 2011. Efficient optimal learning for contextual bandits. In *Proceedings of the Twenty-Seventh Conference on Uncertainty in Artificial Intelligence (UAI'11)*, pp. 169–178. Arlington, VA: AUAI Press.

Elster, J. 1990. Self-interest and altruism. In Mansbridge, J. (ed.), *Against Self-interest.* Elster: Chicago: University of Chicago Press

Eshel, I., Herreiner, D., Samuelson, L., Sansone, E. and Shaked, A. 2000. Cooperation, mimesis, and local interaction. *Sociological Methods and Research* 28(3): 341–364.

Frieden, J. 1999. Actors and preferences in international relations. In Lake, D.A. and Powell, R. (eds.), *Strategic Choice and International Relations.* Frieden: Princeton: Princeton University Press.

Gauthier, D. 1986. *Morals by Agreement.* Oxford: Oxford, Clarendon Press.

Gittins, J.C. 1979. Bandit processes and dynamic allocation indices. *Journal of the Royal Statistical Society. Series B (Methodological)* 41(2): 148–177.

Hobbes, T. 2008. *Leviathan* (J. C. A. Gaskin, Ed.). Oxford: Oxford University Press.
Katehakis, M.N. and Veinott, A.F. 1987. The multi-armed bandit problem: Decomposition and computation. *Mathematics of Operations Research* 12(2): 262–268.
Marvell, G. and Schmitt, D.R. 1968. Are trivial games the most interesting psychologically? *Behavioral Science* 13(2): 125–128.
Maynard Smith, J. 1982. *Evolution and the Theory of Games*. Cambridge: Cambridge University Press.
Maynard Smith, J. and Price, G.R. 1973. The logic of animal conflict. *Nature* 246(5427): 15–18.
Morrow, J. 1994. *Game Theory for Political Scientists*. Princeton, NJ: Princeton University Press.
Nash, J. 1951. Non-cooperative Games. *Annals of Mathematics* 54(2), 286–295.
Osborne, M.J. and Rubinstein, A. 1994. *A Course in Game Theory*. Cambridge, USA: The MIT Press.
Ostrom, E. 1990. *Governing the Commons: The Evolution of Institutions for Collective Action*. New York: Cambridge University Press.
Pareto, V. 1902. Di un nuovo errore nello interpretare le teorie dell'economia matematica (Of a new error in interpreting the theories of mathematical economics). *Giornale degli Economisti*, pp. 401–433.
Robbins, H. 1952. Some aspects of the sequential design of experiments. *Bulletin of the American Mathematical Society* 58(5): 527–535.
Trivers, R.L. 1971. The evolution of reciprocal altruism. *Quarterly Review of Biology* 46(1): 35–57.
Ullmann-Margalit, E. 1977. *The Emergence of Norms*. Oxford: The Clarendon Press.
Vanberg, V. 1994. *Rules and Choice in Economics*. London: Routledge.
Weirich, P. 1998. *Equilibrium and Rationality: Game Theory Revised by Decision Rules*, New York: Cambridge University Press.

Chapter 3

Cooperation

3.1 The Problem of Coordination

In Chapter 2, we discussed noncooperative games and demonstrated how they can be modeled through the application of reinforcement learning. Noncooperative games are one of two broad categories of game theoretic models. In their simplest form, they assume that each player acts independently and pursues their own interests without any communication or coordination with the other players. As we have shown, noncooperative games are often used to model situations where players are primarily motivated by self-interest such as military conflicts. In contrast, in cooperative games, players work together to achieve a common goal, and they can often communicate and/or negotiate with each other to reach mutually beneficial outcomes. Geopolitics of course abounds with examples of cooperative behavior. Well-known examples include the formation of security alliances, the coordination of monetary policy, and the harmonization of trade regimes, among many others.

In game theory, coordination problems arise in cases of multiple equilibria. Individuals coordinate their own actions and in doing so incorporate the expectations of other individuals' actions into their decisions. Other individuals act on their expectations as well, and as a result, decisions become interdependent. When this happens, multiple equilibria can be produced. As an example of how multiple equilibria arise in coordination games, consider two drivers that meet on an empty road. Both have to swerve in order to avoid a head-on collision. If both choose the same side, they manage to pass each

Table 3.1. Pure Coordination: The Driving Game.

		Player 2	
		Left	Right
Player 1	Left	10, 10	0, 0
	Right	0, 0	10, 10

Table 3.2. Battles of the Sexes.

		Player 2	
		Stravinsky	Khachaturian
Player 1	Stravinsky	10, 5	0, 0
	Khachaturian	0, 0	5, 10

other but if they choose different sides they will collide. In the payoff matrix in Table 3.1, the drivers passing each other is represented by a payoff of 10 and a collision is represented by a payoff of 0. In this case, there are two pure Nash equilibria: Either both swerve to the left or both swerve to the right. In this example, it does not matter which side both players pick, as long as they both pick the same one. In other words, both solutions are Pareto efficient.

A coordination game related to the Driving Game is called *Battle of the Sexes*. We show the payoff matrix of the latter game in Table 3.2. In this game, both players want to engage in an activity together, but their preferences differ over which activity they should engage in, for example, what ballet performance they should attend. Player 1 prefers that both see Stravinsky's *The Rite of Spring*, while Player 2 prefers that they attend Khachaturian's *Gayane*. This game has two Nash equilibria, one where both attend *The Rite of Spring* and another where both attend *Gayane*.

The Battle of the Sexes game naturally lends itself to the modeling of many instances of cooperation among international actors. For example, consider the case where the Federal Reserve and the European Central Bank (ECB) have signaled, through public statements, their shared belief that the two banks should act in concert with one another. However, it may also be the case that each central

Table 3.3. Battle of the Central Banks.

		ECB	
		Hike	Maintain
Fed	Hike	10, 5	0, 0
	Maintain	0, 0	5, 10

bank prefers a different specific policy action. The Fed may prefer that the two banks hike interest rates in order to help combat global inflation, while the ECB may prefer that the banks maintain interest rates at their current levels so that global growth is not stymied by a more restrictive monetary policy. As we see in Table 3.3, the foregoing situation perfectly aligns with the payoff structure of the Battle of the Sexes game.

The desire to maintain a coordinated global policy response in this example is but one of many potential drivers of cooperation. Players often cooperate because they believe that they have a higher chance of securing positive payoffs for themselves through the coordination of their actions with others. Agents' belief that cooperation will yield higher payoffs versus acting alone is often connected to an appreciation of their own cognitive limitations. In our discussion of bounded rationality, we noted how limited information-processing capacity serves to constrain human action. Additionally, agents are bound by the time constraints that limit their ability to form and execute optimal decisions. It is unlikely that an individual can either remember or know all the possible combinations of choices that he has at his disposal in a given instance of decision-making. The boundedly rational nature of humans thus implies that the course of action that individuals undertake will inevitably be executed with some degree of inefficiency. Because it is not always possible to choose the "best" course of action available, we are forced to act as satisficers.

However, while satisficing is often taken to be largely a result of our bounded rationality, it would be incorrect to say that cooperation is largely driven by satisficing behavior. Rather, because most human beings do not live in isolation but in collectives of some sort, they must cooperate in order to successfully satisfy many if not most of their individual goals. Cooperation in turn typically constrains individual maximization. We thus arrive at the broadly Hobbesian idea that the reason human beings form stable cooperative relationships in the first place (i.e., "enter a social contract") is because they have to out of necessity, i.e., because they are constrained maximizers. Cooperation then, can be viewed as an adaptation that individuals develop because of environmental challenges that they cannot overcome alone. We discuss this idea in the next section.

3.2 The Origin of Cooperation II: Evidence from Nature

As we discussed in Chapter 1, the natural world provides a useful guide for understanding the origins of cooperation. Thus, to understand the formation and maintenance of cooperative structures, it seems reasonable to look to the domain of non-human animals as a first source. Biologists, like economists, generally see cooperation as an anomalous phenomenon, as it is assumed that living in groups is detrimental to an animal's survival because it exposes them to competitors for resources. Such competition can result in injury and death and is extremely costly in terms of energy expenditure. Nevertheless, social groups do form. The question is, "Why?"

Biologists have amassed an overwhelming amount of evidence on a wide range of organisms, from bacteria to mole rats, that explains cooperative behavior as a response to environmental adversity. Adversity can come in the form of predators, harsh weather, competitors for food, or any other entity or phenomenon present in an environment that puts an organism's survival at risk.[1] A large amount of field research on various animals, primates, for example, also supports the claim that environmental adversity promotes the development of cooperative modes of behavior within species. With primate species, field studies[2] have pointed to two primary motivators that lead to cooperation: (1) In cases where the frequency of predation is high in a given environment, primates will tend to band together for defensive purposes. The reason is simple: The more animals there are, the more eyes available for surveillance. The need

---

[1] Andras and Lazarus (2005).
[2] See for example, Wrangham (1980), Janson (1990), Isbell (1994), Isbell and Young (1993), Bshary and Noe (1997), Noe and Bshary (1997), and McGraw and Bshary (2002).

for "lookouts" is particularly acute in environments without foliage (e.g., savannahs), where animals can hide. (2) Primates tend to band together in order to better compete with other members of their species for food in a given foraging area. Thus, an area with a high density of members of the same species will be more likely to have social formations than a thinly populated area. Conversely, when predation and resource competition are at relatively low levels, a solitary lifestyle tends to develop, as is the case with orangutans. Biology thus paints a picture where cooperation among members of a species is a necessity, and cooperators view each other as means to facilitate the individual acquisition of resources.

Indeed, in nature, much of cooperative behavior can ultimately be traced to self-interest. Consider the examples presented by Brian Skyrms.[3] One is the kamikaze behavior of worker bees that "selflessly" give their lives for the sake of their hive. The view that worker bees are acting for the collective good for motives other than self-interest (e.g., due to some sense of altruism) becomes less tenable once it is pointed out that they are sterile and cannot pass on their genes even if they survive. There is thus much to be gained by worker bees in protecting their relatives in the hive who can reproduce and pass on genes that the workers share with them. There is nothing to be gained and much to be lost by individual worker bees that look out for themselves. In other parts of the animal world, we can also observe many instances of seemingly altruistic behavior that can be more plausibly described as serving the self-interest of individual animals.[4] For example, Skyrms mentions that the alarm calls given by various animals may appear to be instances of altruism. Skyrms depicts this behavior as one where some animals imperil themselves in order to alert the other members of their group to the presence of predators. But there are various non-altruistic explanations for this behavior. For one, most members of an animal's group are likely to be related to it (i.e., they are engaging in "kin cooperation"). Thus, they have an evolutionary interest in protecting animals that they share genes with, as in the case of the worker bees. Moreover, some animals are noisy or display other types of conspicuous behavior.

---

[3]Skyrms (1996, 2004).
[4]Dawkins (1976).

An individual animal that spots a predator but stays silent will not be doing himself any good, because if the other group members remain conspicuous, the predator will still notice the group, including the individual giving the alarm call. Also, if an animal chooses to be the "odd man out" and breaks away on his own, he may attract attention to himself. However, if the entire group escapes at once, the predator's attention will be diverted in many directions not just toward one animal. Thus, self-interest is at work here as well.

Skyrms has further argued that the game known as the Stag Hunt (SH) most faithfully represents how cooperation evolved. In the SH, two individuals go out on a hunt. Each can choose to hunt a stag or a hare. The two individuals must choose which animal to hunt without knowing the other's choice. Now, if an individual wants to successfully hunt a stag, he requires the cooperation of the other individual. An individual can successfully hunt a hare by himself, but since a hare is worth less than a stag, it is thought that individuals will be induced to cooperate by the promise of a larger payoff. The payoff structure of the SH is illustrated in Table 3.4.

The SH differs from the Prisoner's Dilemma in that in the SH there are two pure-strategy Nash equilibria, one where both players cooperate and one where both players defect. In contrast, in the Prisoner's Dilemma, despite the fact that both players cooperating is Pareto optimal, the only pure Nash equilibrium is when both players choose to defect.

The SH models the conflict between playing it safe and assuring oneself of a smaller payoff and taking a risk for the possibility of a higher payoff. The primary risk individuals face in the SH is one of trust. If an individual chooses to cooperate and hunt a stag but the other player does not, he assumes the role of a "sucker" and

Table 3.4. Stag Hunt.

		Player 2 Stag	Hare
Player 1	Stag	5, 5	−1, 3
	Hare	3, −1	3, 3

gets a negative payoff because no one can successfully hunt a stag alone. Thus, there is an assurance problem. In the SH, cooperation is seen as providing a higher payoff in the form of more food, provided that the assurance problem is solved. The game can serve as an analogy for social cooperation because in society much of the benefit that community members enjoy depends on cooperating with other people, which in turn demands that individuals trust one another to achieve collective ends.

SH scenarios are frequently encountered in international affairs. For example, consider Brexit, a concrete example of a SH. During Brexit, the United Kingdom, through a referendum, decided to defect from the EU, electing instead to independently "hunt a hare." In doing so, the UK expressed its belief that there was a higher probability of securing political and economic gains for itself without formal policy coordination with the EU. Some other prominent examples of the SH in international affairs include compliance with the Nuclear Non-Proliferation Treaty (NPT), an international treaty aimed at preventing the spread of nuclear weapons. Here, collective security is the stag and the individual acquisition of nuclear weapons is the hare. Yet another example would be cooperating with and adhering to the directives of transnational security organizations like NATO (North Atlantic Treaty Organization). In organizations like NATO, member states must decide between pursuing their individual security interests and cooperating with other members to ensure collective security. Choosing to hunt a stag in this context would be analogous to all members upholding their shared commitments and forming a united front against potential aggressors. However, if one member decides to pursue a hare and satisfy its individual security interests in violation of its obligations, it can weaken the alliance and put other members at risk. We have seen an example of the latter behavior in the case of Turkey, which has pursued individual security relations with, for example, Russia, a country that is antagonistic toward NATO.

The SH represents one way of interpreting observed cooperative behavior. However, another interpretation of the benefit of cooperation views it as beneficial for animal species not because it increases the number of resources available to individual animals but because it increases the probability that they will secure resources *at all*. This is in contrast to the SH, in which cooperation is the riskier endeavor

Table 3.5. Evolutionarily Committed Cooperators.

		Player 2	
		Cooperate	Defect
Player 1	Cooperate	1, 1	0, 0
	Defect	0, 0	0, 0

and going it alone the safer bet. In nature, the assurance problem that plagues the SH is not always present, because when animal species form cooperative structures, they often do it out of necessity, as going it alone can be "evolutionary suicide" in a given environment. Moreover, cooperation usually does not bring more resources to the individual members of a species but less, because when social groups do form, animals must share resources with other members. They nevertheless become evolutionarily *committed* to cooperation because they have to in order to survive. The payoff matrix for such *evolutionarily committed cooperators* is shown in Table 3.5.

In Table 3.5, cooperation on the part of both players is the only action combination with positive payoffs, consistent with the scenario where high levels of external selective pressures in the form of high levels of predation and/or resource competition make cooperation the only way in which organisms can acquire any amount of resources for themselves.[5]

It is important to remember that when deciding which type of game accurately describes a particular instance of cooperation, we must consider what actions would be considered *rational* by the players. In the natural world, what actions are considered rational depends on the environment. Any behavior that allows an organism to survive, reproduce, and pass on its genes qualifies as rational. Survival is also the goal of human beings, but instead of the natural environment as the determiner of what is rational, it is more often the social/institutional context that allows us to confidently judge an action as rational or irrational. This is captured by Sunstein's idea of a social role, which we described in Chapter 1.

---

[5]There is some similarity to the game depicted in Table 3.5 and the "mortar men" variation of the Prisoner's Dilemma discussed in Chapter 2.

3.3 Modeling Cooperative Games Using CMABs

In games involving cooperation, we can also invoke the formal machinery of bandit algorithms. As with noncooperative games, the application of CMABs gives us the ability to vary the size of the payoffs as well as the respective probability values assigned to cooperation and defection in different contexts. For example, consider the alternative payoff matrix for the SH shown in Table 3.6, where we have increased the perceived costs to non-coordination and reduced the gap between cooperating and going it alone.

Let us run through an implementation of the SH using the payoff matrices in Tables 3.4 and 3.6 as our varying types (contexts). Our implementation begins with an assignment of probabilities to payoffs in a given context. In our example, we assign a probability of 0.65 that the Stag is perceived as "High Value" as in Table 3.4 and a probability of 0.35 that the Stag is perceived as "Low Value" as in Table 3.6. Next, we assign probabilities that cooperation will occur given the Stag's type. We assign a 0.65 probability that Player 1 will choose to cooperate if the Stag is High Value and a 0.60 probability that Player 1 will choose to cooperate if the Stag is Low Value. The payoff for the Hare is set to a constant value of 3. The Hare thus serves as a convenient reference with which to judge the utility of cooperation. The use of a constant value for the Hare also results in a computationally simpler game.

In Figure 3.1, we see that the Hare receives a higher long-run average payoff, despite the high probability values assigned to both the Stag being High Value and the likelihood of cooperation regardless of the Stag's type.

One of the defining features of the SH is that there is an action, pursuing the Hare, which does not have any uncertainty with regard

Table 3.6. Stag Hunt 2.

		Player 2	
		Stag	Hare
Player 1	Stag	4, 4	−2, 3
	Hare	3, −2	3, 3

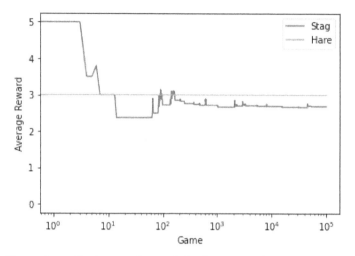

Figure 3.1. Evolution of Payoffs for Stag Hunt (First Iteration).

to securing a payoff. Thus, while the payoff for the Hare is considerably lower than for the Stag, the absence of uncertainty in securing a payoff makes the Hare a compelling choice for any player. In contrast, in a game like the Run–Pass game, the players face payoff uncertainty in taking either action. This is an important distinction if we take the view, as Skyrms does, that the SH is the primary template for cooperation. If cooperation depends on rejecting an action with a certain payoff in favor of an action with an uncertain payoff, then the payoff for the action with uncertainty attached to it needs to be sufficiently high to motivate its selection. The latter state of affairs, if true, neatly captures the challenge of cooperation. To see just how important the payoff value is in inducing cooperation in the SH, we rerun the simulation and adjust the payoff for the High Value Stag type to 6. All the other input parameters are unchanged, including the Stag's payoff for its Low Value type. We show the results in Figure 3.2. As we can see in the figure, our upward adjustment to the payoff for the High Value Stag has a noticeable impact on Stag's long-term average reward value.

Next, we run the simulation a third time, but do not change the payoff for the High Value Stag. Instead, we adjust the probability of the Stag being High Value upward to 1. As we see in Figure 3.3, even when the Stag is guaranteed to be High Value, the Hare still

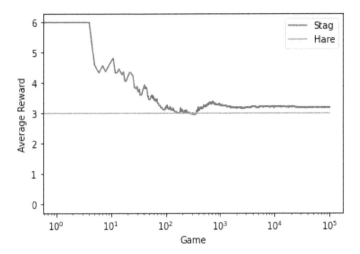

Figure 3.2. Evolution of Payoffs for Stag Hunt (Second Iteration).

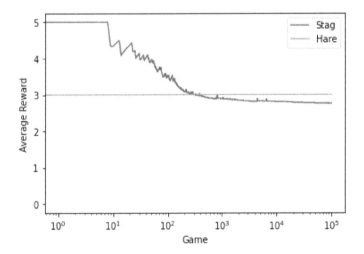

Figure 3.3. Evolution of Payoffs for Stag Hunt (Third Iteration).

delivers a higher average payoff. It is only when we further upwardly adjust Player 1's probability of cooperation *given* the Stag being of High Value that the Stag produces a higher long-run average payoff. To illustrate the latter point, in Figure 3.4, we show the average payoffs for each action under the assumption that Player 1 has a 0.75 probability of choosing Stag when it is High Value, an occurrence

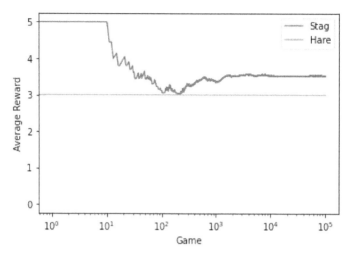

Figure 3.4. Evolution of Payoffs for Stag Hunt (Fourth Iteration).

which we again assume has a probability of 1. As the figure shows, when we assign very high probability values in favor of both the Stag being High Value and cooperation, we see that the average long-run payoff for choosing the Stag does indeed exceed that of choosing Hare.

What normative conclusion can we draw from these simulations? Well, if we interpret "the probability to cooperate" as an expression of an agent's inclination or desire to cooperate, then the simulations tell us that even if agents have the inclination to cooperate, they *should not* cooperate if the measurable benefits do not justify it. Put another way, inducing cooperation is *hard*. As we see in our different iterations of the game, the probability of cooperation values must be very high in order to nudge Stag ahead of Hare in terms of their long-run average payoffs, while simply raising the Stag's High Value payoff by one unit (and keeping its Low Value payoff the same) is enough to make Stag the higher payoff action in the long-run. In international relations, we unfortunately often see the difficulty in establishing cooperative outcomes, as evidenced by the many instances of parties to a negotiation failing to come to an agreement on some substantive matter despite the fact that they have expressed their sincere desire to cooperate. This type of breakdown in cooperation reflects the self-interested rationality of the agents involved in the negotiation, because they presumably understand that as much as they want to come to an agreement, it may not be beneficial for them to do so. If one of the potential parties to an agreement cooperates even if it is not in their interest to do so (perhaps under pressure by mediators or the other parties to the agreement), there is a good chance that the agreement may be violated in the future. One historical example of the latter type of cooperation breakdown is the ultimate demise of the General Agreement on Tariffs and Trade (GATT) signed in 1947. The GATT was created to promote international trade and reduce tariffs. However, many countries eventually violated GATT rules by imposing tariffs and other trade barriers when they were in a position to do so. The degradation of the GATT regime over time could be interpreted as a breakdown of cooperation in an iterated Stag Hunt, similar to that illustrated in the simulations where the payoffs for Stag are not high enough to outweigh the probability that the other player (or players in the case of the GATT) will eventually view Hare as the more desirable choice.

3.4 Determining Whether an Agreement Is Fair

Cooperation in general and international agreements in particular often focus on the division of resources of some type. In the SH game discussed in the previous section, we simply posited payoffs to cooperation (Stag) under the implicit assumption that each player will share the Stag equally. However, this is often not the case in actual instances of cooperation. That is, establishing and maintaining cooperation often does not require that resources be split equally among the individuals that are a party to an agreement. Rather, the portion of resources that is allocated to each party will be based on a number of factors, especially their initial (presumably rightful) claims at the outset of negotiations.

It would be useful if there was a formal methodology to help us determine if an allocation of resources is fair given the initial claims of the negotiating parties. Knowing what a fair allocation is would give us some indication of the likelihood that cooperation is going to persist or collapse based on some perceived unfairness on the part of one or more of the parties. But how do we determine if an agreement is fair? Well, as a first step, we can try and find a solution that allocates resources based on widely accepted notions of rationality and collective utility. Luckily, the bargaining solution known as the Shapley value (SV) allocates resources in precise conformance with the latter criteria. The SV is a game theoretic solution to the problem of resource (or cost) allocation introduced by Lloyd Shapley (1953) for the theory of cooperative games.[6] Shapley introduced the solution as a way for players to assess *a priori* the benefits that they would individually gain from cooperating. The SV is driven by the goal of producing a fair outcome, aiming to distribute the payoff of a game among the players in an equitable manner. It considers the individual contributions of the players as well as the cooperative nature of the game. To calculate the SV, all possible orderings of the players are considered, and for each ordering, the marginal contribution of each player is determined. The SV is then obtained by averaging these marginal contributions across all possible orderings.

The degree to which the outcome of a negotiation, as reflected in a final allocation of resources, rights, or privileges, is considered fair by the parties involved is an important determinant of whether an agreement is likely to hold or be violated sometime in the future by one of the parties to it. For investors, gauging the durability of an international agreement is important to their deliberations over the likely course of events in different countries and regions. If they determine that a particular international agreement is not likely to hold, then they may refrain from investing in countries and regions affected by the agreement in question.

We begin our formal description of the SV by first defining a transferable utility game (TUG). Let $N = \{1, 2, \ldots, n\}$ be a set of *players*, $|N| = n$, and $v : 2^N \to \mathbb{R}$ a function satisfying $v(\emptyset) = 0$, where 2^N is the set of all subsets of N. We denote by the pair (N, v) a TUG with a player set N. For any coalition $S \subseteq N$, $v(S)$ is called

---

[6]There have also been financial applications of the Shapley value. Mussard and Terraza (2008) apply the Shapley value to the decomposition of portfolio risk. Simonian (2012) applies the solution to the problem of aggregating multiple investment views. Simonian (2014) builds on the latter work and uses the Shapley value to solve the problem of aggregating sets of interconnected probability estimates in a logically coherent manner. Simonian (2019) demonstrates how the Shapley value can be used as a type of shrinkage operator and as a substitute for traditional portfolio optimization.

the *worth* of S. Denote by G^N the space of games with a finite player set N. Given a game (N,v) and a coalition S, we write (S,v) for the subgame obtained by restricting v to subsets of S only. We further define a *value* as a function ψ which assigns a real number $\psi_i(N,v)$ to every game (N,v) and every player $i \in N$.

To derive the SV, we let $\Omega(N)$ be the set of all orders in N. Any $\omega \in \Omega(N)$ is a bijection from N to $\{1,2,\ldots,n\} |N| = n$, and $\omega(i) < \omega(j)$ signifies that player i comes before player j in the ordering ω. We denote by P_ω^i the set of predecessors of i in ω, i.e., $P_\omega^i := (j \in N : \omega(j) < \omega(i))$. Further, the *marginal contribution* that every player i receives in any ordering ω is defined by

$$m_i^\omega = (N,v) := v(P_\omega^i \cup i) - v(P_\omega^i), \qquad (3.1)$$

$$\phi_i(N,v) = \frac{1}{n!} \sum_{\omega \in \Omega(N)} m_i^\omega(N,v), \ (i \in N). \qquad (3.2)$$

Thus, the SV is the payoff $\phi_i(N,v)$ that player i expects to obtain in v if, for any possible order ω, where all orders are equally likely, i is rewarded with i's marginal contribution to P_ω^i.

The SV is attractive as an aggregation mechanism because it possesses properties that are supportive of a robust conception of collective reasoning. Specifically, the SV is bound by the following axioms:

Efficiency : $\sum_{i \in N} \phi_i(v) = v(N).$ \hfill (3.3)

Symmetry : $v(S \cup \{i\}) = v(S \cup \{j\})$, for every S of N. \hfill (3.4)

Additivity : $\phi_i(v+w) = \phi_i(v) + \phi_i(w).$ \hfill (3.5)

Null Player : i is null in v if $v(S \cup Z\{i\}) = v(S)$ for all S. \hfill (3.6)

To see how the SV can be applied in geopolitical analysis, let us consider an example. Suppose we have a maritime dispute between four nations A, B, C, and D. Each claims a percentage of gas fields located in the oceanic waters that are shared by the claimants. We can assume that the countries base their claim on information gleaned from a number of historical maps and their past individual use patterns. We further assume that the maps are not perfectly aligned in their demarcation of the body of water in question and also that the countries' historical use of underwater resources has overlapped. Thus, an objective and fair solution is needed to resolve the issue. We assume that the initial individual country claims are A: 55%, B: 65%, C: 55%, and D: 75%. Thus, it is impossible to satisfy each of the party's claims in full. However, by applying the SV solution described above, we get the following feasible (and presumably fair) allocation: A: 22%, B: 26%, C: 22%, and D: 30%.

3.5 Stable Cooperative Structures

Establishing cooperation is but the first step in the formation of collective action. Maintaining the stability of cooperative structures is no less important. To this end, we may utilize various types of algorithmic frameworks to analyze the robustness of cooperative relationships, including those in the geopolitical realm. For example, it is possible to apply what is known as the *Gale–Shapley algorithm* (Gale and Shapley, 1962) to the analysis of alliance formation among states. The algorithm is well known for its application to the stable marriage problem and the related hospital–resident problem. In the stable marriage problem, the algorithm is used to determine what configuration of pairings from two equal-sized sets of individuals will exhibit the most stability given their preferences for being matched with members of the opposing set. Formally, a match is a bijection from the elements of one set to the elements of another set. A match is in turn considered stable when there does not exist any match that the members prefer over an existing match. The hospital–resident problem is a more general version of the stable marriage problem, allowing one set (hospitals) to be matched with more than one element from the opposing set (residents). The formal solution to solving the alliance formation variant of the hospital–resident problem is described in Algorithm 3.1. The hospital–resident problem is similar to alliance formation among states where what we will call "greater powers" are somewhat analogous to hospitals that have the capacity to ally with several countries that we call "lesser powers." While any kind of alliance formation is presumably of interest to macro investors, consideration of economic alliances is often central to the formation of market views. Economic alliances are often formed when greater powers offer economic aid, trade preferences, or direct investment to lesser powers in exchange for economic and/or political concessions

Algorithm 3.1 Alliance formation algorithm.

We consider two distinct sets, L and G, which represent what we call lesser powers and greater powers, respectively. Each greater power $g \in G$ has the capacity $c_g \in \mathbb{N}$ to accommodate a finite number of lesser powers:

1. Each lesser power $l \in L$ must rank a non-empty subset of G. We denote this preference by $p(l)$.
2. Each greater power $g \in G$ must rank all lesser powers under consideration for alliance formation. Thus, the preference list of l, denoted by $p(g)$, is a permutation of the set given by $\{l \in L\} | g \in p(l)\}$.[7]

A matching M is any mapping between L and G. If a pair $(l, g) \in L \times G$ is matched in M, we say that $M(l) = g$ and $l \in M^{-1}(g)$. A match is considered valid if all of the following are satisfied:

3. For all $l \in L$ with a match, we have $M(r) \in p(l)$.
4. For all $g \in G$ with matches, we have $M^{-1}(g) \subseteq p(g)$.
5. For all $g \in G$, we have $|M^{-1}(g) \leq c_g|$.

A valid match M is considered stable if it does not contain a *blocking pair* (r, h), which is defined thus:

6. There is mutual preference: $l \in p(g) \wedge g \in p(l)$.
7. Either l is unmatched or prefers g to $M(l) = g'$.
8. Either $|M^{-1}(g) < c_g|$ or g prefers l to at least one $l' \in M^{-1}(g)$.

(e.g., favorable terms for natural resource extraction, basing rights). Their choice of what lesser powers to ally with could also be based on a number of political considerations such as geography or similar political ideologies, among others.

As an example, consider a situation where we have three greater powers (GP) and five lesser powers (LP). Let us assume that the

---

[7] It is possible for a lesser power to leave a greater power unranked and thereby remove it from consideration as an ally. However, we assume that all lesser powers do in fact rank every greater power. This serves to simplify our exposition but is also arguably a more realistic characterization of lesser powers' behavior given their need for support from a stronger country.

respective rankings of each of the greater and lesser powers are as follows: GP1: {LP2, LP5, LP1, LP4, LP3}, GP2: {LP3, LP5, LP4}, GP3: {LP2, LP4, LP1, LP5}, LP1: {GP3, GP1, GP2}, LP2: {GP3, GP1, GP2}, LP3: {GP2, GP1, GP3}, LP4: {GP3, GP2, GP1}, LP5: {GP1, GP2, GP3}. We further assume that each greater power only has the resources to undertake alliances with two lesser powers. Using Algorithm 3.1, we come to the following set of matches: GP1: {LP2, LP3}, GP2: {LP4}, GP3: {None}. As we see by the results, LP1 and LP5 are not matched with any greater power, while GP1 is matched with two lesser powers.

How would we use the foregoing type of analysis in an investment context? Well, the preferences attributed to each respective greater or lesser power presumably derive from research on the economic strengths and challenges of each of the countries under consideration. The alliance preferences of countries are also often revealed by their behavior. For example, countries will often pass legislation to harmonize the relevant parts of their economies with potential partners. Based on the foregoing, if we assume confidence in the assigned preferences, then the application of the Gale–Shapely algorithm can be further assumed to give us an accurate characterization of the equilibrium alliance structure. With this information in hand, we can observe the countries' economic relations over time and, as events play out, determine if they are unfolding in a manner that is likely to bode well or ill for the stability of the various alliances considered. These observations can then be used to fill out a more comprehensive assessment of a country's economic prospects over a specified investment horizon.

The Gale–Shapely algorithm could be applied to analyzing other instances of economically relevant cooperation, for example, the coordination of monetary policy. If we assume that we have a set of central banks from large-economy countries on the one hand and a set of central banks from small-economy countries on the other, we can "match" each large-economy central bank with one or more small-economy central banks to determine whether observed policy coordination behavior is likely to result in a stable global monetary equilibrium.

Another solution that allows us to gauge the stability of cooperative structures is the Myerson value (MV) (Myerson, 1977). While similar to the SV, the MV puts more emphasis on the stability of cooperative structures, as it provides a way to allocate the payoff of a game to the players such that no subset of players has the incentive to form a new coalition and deviate from the allocated solution. The calculation of the MV involves determining the payoff of the game for each possible coalition, in light of the different bargaining powers or leverage of the players.

The MV is of obvious relevance to analyzing international relations, as various types of political negotiations between countries often involve asymmetric bargaining powers and run the risk of unstable outcomes. For example, when countries engage in trade negotiations, each country aims to secure the best possible terms and benefits for themselves. The MV can be applied in this context to determine the optimal allocation of trade benefits given the differing bargaining powers of the countries that are parties to the negotiations. A country's bargaining power will generally be a function of its economic size, market access, and political and military influence. By applying the MV, we can determine what allocation of resources will be maximally stable given the respective bargaining strength of each negotiating party. Mathematically, the MV can be defined as follows:

Let $N = \{1, 2, \ldots, n\}$ be the set of players in a cooperative game, and let $v(S)$ be the characteristic function that represents the worth of each coalition $S \subseteq N$. The MV for player i is denoted by φi and can be expressed as follows:

$$\varphi i(v) = \sum w(S) \cdot \delta i(S), \tag{3.7}$$

where the summation is taken over all coalitions $S \subseteq N$ that include player i. The term $w(S)$ represents the worth of coalition S, which is defined as the characteristic function value $v(S)$. The bargaining power $\delta i(S)$ of player i in coalition S represents the average contribution of player i to all possible coalitions containing i. Again, the inclusion of bargaining power allows for a more nuanced evaluation of the worth of a coalition in light of the relative influence of the players. Thus, the MV with bargaining power for a player is the weighted average difference in worth that the player contributes to each coalition it participates in, compared to the worth of the same coalition without that player.

Players with higher bargaining power will, all things being equal, receive a greater share of the total worth. In addition to bargaining power, we may also include *reservation values* (or *reservation prices*) for each player. Reservation values represent the minimum acceptable offers that each player is willing to accept in a bargaining situation. It is the threshold below which a player would be inclined to reject an offer rather than accept it. If one or more players is allocated less than their reservation value, it could be an indication that the solution is unstable.

Let us return to the example we used to illustrate the SV in order to observe the various dimensions of the MV solution. We assume that the individual country reservation values are equivalent to their claims in the previous example where we illustrated the derivation of the SV: A: 55%, B: 65%, C: 55%, and D: 75%. But now, we also assume that the players have different levels of bargaining power. For the relative bargaining powers of the players, we assume the following values: A: 0.3, B: 0.2, C: 0.5, and D: 0.4. Given these inputs, we arrive at the following final allocation: A: 18.97%, B: 14.94%, C: 31.61%, and D: 34.48%. As we can see by the results, players' bargaining power has a significant impact on the final allocation, in some cases overriding the relative allocation implied by players' reservation values. We see this in the present example with players A and B. Player A is given a higher allocation of resources even though Player B has a (presumably justified) higher reservation value than Player A. We further note that, as in this example, players' bargaining power is also often a driver of more concentrated outcomes compared to the SV. Indeed, in our MV example, the players with the most bargaining power, C and D, are given a disproportionate share of resources relative to their allocations in the SV example discussed earlier: A: 22%, B: 26%, C: 22%, and D: 30%.

3.6 Guided Cooperation: Correlated Equilibrium

Thus far in this chapter, we have presented and analyzed formal models of cooperation. While the establishment of international cooperation always requires communication to some degree, it is often hindered by gamesmanship, diplomatic protocol, and/or regulations barring explicit coordination among stakeholders. Given that this is the case, individual agents often need the assistance of an external signal to guide them toward cooperative outcomes.

The concept of a *correlated equilibrium* introduced by Aumann (1974) provides a game-theoretic articulation of the latter type of signal. Correlated equilibrium is a refinement of the concept of Nash equilibrium, where each player's strategy is the best response to the strategies chosen by the other players. In establishing a correlated equilibrium, players receive a signal, known as the *correlating device*, that helps them select their strategies in a coordinated manner. These signals provide probabilistic or conditional information about their choices. The signals can be public or private, revealing some information that players use to adjust their strategies. Correlated equilibria thus facilitate coordination among players without direct communication on their part.

As an example of correlated equilibrium, consider the case where two central banks, while setting monetary policy independently, would like to coordinate their actions. They are, however, barred by their respective governments from explicitly coordinating or communicating policy decisions with other central banks before they are publicly announced. Now, assume that the International Monetary Fund (IMF) releases a report on global economic conditions and provides a recommendation for central bank interest rate policy based on its outlook for the global economy. In this case, the IMF, as a credible and trustworthy institution, acts as a correlating device for the two central banks (and others presumably). Each central bank, conditioned on the received signals, independently chooses its respective policy rate and thereby helps to drive stable economic conditions globally.

A concept related to correlated equilibrium is the idea of *focal points* discussed by Schelling (1960) within the framework of solving coordination games in situations where there is no communication among players. Unlike correlated equilibrium, focal points do not involve the use of signals or a correlating device to guide players' choices. Rather, focal points refer to the intuitive choices that players might converge on due to their salience to the strategic context, even in the absence of an external signal.[8] Schelling argues that when focal

---

[8]Focal points in turn bear some relation to conventions, but the two concepts are not identical. What differentiates focal points from conventions is that focal points are psychological anchors that agents may not be aware of, while conventions are rules that individuals consciously conform to. Conventions can arise

points exist, games of coordination without communication are more likely to end up in socially desirable equilibria and thereby solve the collective action ("state of nature") problem. As an example, one of the scenarios that Schelling presents is where two strangers are told to meet in New York City but have not communicated with each other regarding the location of the meeting. Schelling posits that in this situation there are certain solutions, like meeting at Grand Central Station, that will implicitly present themselves to individuals. Schelling argues that in situations where cooperation is desired but explicit communication is impossible, focal points can and often do serve as the psychological anchors needed to get people to arrive at a coordinated outcome.

Strategically, the importance of correlating devices with regard to the construction and maintenance of societal order emanates from the fact that they serve to remove three basic obstacles to cooperation in positive-sum games: (1) information costs, (2) the transaction costs of cooperation, and (3) uncertainty. In the realm of international relations, mutually advantageous agreements are often stymied by the fact that individuals cannot efficiently secure information about what others are doing, they cannot efficiently communicate and coordinate with others, and they are uncertain about whether others will honor their agreements. The existence of correlating devices makes the behavior of others more predictable.

In positive-sum games, individuals have an incentive to cooperate to the degree that others cooperate. For this reason, correlating devices will make behavior much more predictable and minimize the need to obtain information about the behavior of others or communicate with others. Indeed, correlating devices will minimize uncertainty regarding cooperation breakdown as the presence of a mutually recognized correlating device will give agents assurance that they are headed toward a common end. Thus, in certain situations, there is no

---

spontaneously or through a conscious consensus among members of a group. But one property that all conventions share is that they all supply mutual expectations of the behavior of those who are affected by them. By applying conventions, individuals can direct themselves to act in certain ways without much deliberation. Moreover, by detecting the application of conventions in others, they can form expectations of others' actions.

apparatus that is as effective as a correlating device for eliminating the aforementioned challenges to cooperation.

3.7 Concluding Points

In Chapters 2 and 3, the roots of rational decision-making in games of conflict and cooperation were presented and analyzed as contextual multi-armed bandit problems. While bandit problems allow us to gain insight into an agent's optimal actions in the face of uncertainty, they are nevertheless somewhat simplified frameworks where an agent's actions do not influence the realization of states over multiple iterations. In contrast, "true" reinforcement learning algorithms analyze decision-making problems in interactive environments where an agent's action can shape the state of the world they find themselves in. Geopolitical interaction is often interactive in this way. In addition, international relations often involve nuanced temporal dynamics between agents. Accordingly, in Chapter 4, we will examine strategic interaction from the standpoint of Q-learning, a reinforcement learning algorithm ideally suited to analyzing games with more complex interactive dynamics.

References

Aumann, R. 1974. Subjectivity and correlation in randomized strategies. *Journal of Mathematical Economics* 1(1): 67–96.

Andras, P. and Lazarus, J. 2005. Cooperation, risk and the evolution of teamwork. In Gold, N. (ed.), *Teamwork: Multi-disciplinary Perspectives*. Palgrave Macmillan London.

Bshary, R. and Noe, R. 1997. Red colobus and Diana monkeys provide mutual protection against predators. *Animal Behavior* 54: 1461–1474.

Dawkins, R. 1976. *The Selfish Gene*. Oxford: Oxford University Press.

Gale, D. and Shapley, L.S. 1962. College admissions and the stability of marriage. *American Mathematical Monthly* 69(1): 9–14.

Isbell, L.A. 1994. Predation on primates: Ecological patterns and evolutionary consequences. *Evolutionary Anthropology* 3(2): 61–71.

Isbell, L.A. and Young, T.P. 1993. Social and ecological influences on activity budgets of Vervet monkeys and their implications for group living. *Behavioral Ecology and Sociobiology* 32: 377–385.

Janson, C.H. 1990. Ecological consequences of individual spatial choice in foraging groups of brown Capuchin monkeys *Cebus apella*. *Animal Behavior* 40: 922–934.

Myerson, R. 1977. Graphs and cooperation in games. *Mathematics of Operations Research* 2(3): 225–229.

Mussard, S. and Terraza, V. 2008. The Shapley decomposition for portfolio risk. *Applied Economics Letters* 15(9): 713–715.

Noe, R. and Bshary, R. 1997. The formation of Red colobus-Diana monkey associations under predation pressure from chimpanzees. *Proceedings of the Royal Society of London (B) Biological Science* 264(1379): 253–259.

Schelling, T. 1960. *The Strategy of Conflict*. Cambridge: Harvard University Press.

Shapley, L.S. 1953. A value for n-person games. In Kuhn, H. and Tucker, A.W. (eds.), *Contributions to the Theory of Games II*, pp. 307–317. Princeton, NJ: Princeton University Press.

Simonian, J. 2012. A formal methodology for aggregating multiple market views. *Applied Financial Economics* 22(14): 1175–1179.

Simonian, J. 2014. Copula-opinion pooling with complex opinions. *Quantitative Finance* 14(6): 941–946.

Simonian, J. 2019. Portfolio selection: A game-theoretic approach. *The Journal of Portfolio Management* 45(6): 108–116.

Skyrms, B. 1996. *Evolution of the Social Contract*. Cambridge: Cambridge University Press.

Skyrms, B. 2004. *The Stag Hunt and the Evolution of Social Structure*. Cambridge: Cambridge University Press.

Chapter 4

Games with Complex Interaction

4.1 Learning in International Relations

Geopolitical actors have to contend with many considerations. First and foremost, they have to take stock of their actions and the actions of their partners and adversaries. Then, over time, they must update their decision-making policies given new information garnered from repeated interactions with others. A truly accurate account of strategic interaction must thus account for the complex temporal dynamics in play in both conflict and cooperation. In the previous two chapters, we provided game theoretic models with a significant degree of analytical depth. Our presentation of games of incomplete information within the contextual multi-armed bandit (CMAB) algorithm allowed us to build informative simulations of various games and provided us with a base from which to explore additional dimensions of strategic interaction.

However, one of the shortcomings of the CMAB algorithm is that it is not ideal for analyzing sequential decision-making, which can be an important aspect of realistically modeling various situations, including in geopolitics. CMABs are thus better suited for analyzing shorter-term decision-making in uncertain environments. But perhaps the most fundamental shortcoming of CMABs is that while they have a notion of a *state* via their use of contexts, the agents in a CMAB can only influence the rewards (payoffs) they receive in a given state. They cannot, through their actions, influence what state they are in during a subsequent episode of decision-making. This is an important analytical gap in CMAB models because in many cases, building realistic models requires that agents possess the latter ability. For example, major central banks like the Fed may find themselves in various macroeconomic states, but they also have the ability to influence the future macroeconomic states that they (and possibly other central banks) find themselves in by the actions they take. A related point is that in many situations, such as interstate negotiations, dealing with the uncertainties related to the transitions between states in partially observable environments is important. CMABs are generally not equipped to handle state transitions in the required manner.

Given the importance of the foregoing considerations, in this chapter, we will draw upon a reinforcement learning algorithm known as *Q-learning* that we will use to model a new set of games. Q-learning and CMABs are both reinforcement learning frameworks, but they have different strengths with regard to their ability to effectively model strategic interaction. In contrast to the CMAB framework, Q-learning is well suited for more complex games where decisions are made sequentially and thus require agents to consider the long-term consequences of their actions. It is especially useful in situations where the optimal action may not be immediately apparent and may depend on the history of previous actions and states. Q-learning is also better at processing environments where agents can influence what state they transition to and where the interactions between agents and/or states exhibit a high degree of intricacy. As we shall see, Q-learning is designed to handle the uncertainties inherent in state transitions due to its ability to estimate future rewards based on observed transitions. In particular, Q-learning algorithms have the ability to balance between exploring new states and exploiting known information in such a way that they can often generate optimal decisions even in the face of significant environmental uncertainty.

4.2 Q-learning

Q-learning navigates complex state transitions by utilizing *Markov Decision Processes* (MDPs).[1] A MDP is a mathematical framework

---

[1] Seminal papers in the development of Q-learning include Watkins and Dayan (1992), Tesauro (1995), Hasselt (2010), Schulman, *et al.* (2015), Hasselt *et al.* (2016), Wang *et al.* (2016), and Ha and Schmidhuber (2018).

used to model decision-making in situations where outcomes are influenced by both random events and the actions taken by a decision-maker. In a MDP, the decision-making process consists of a set of possible states that the system can be in and a set of possible actions that the decision-maker can take. The available actions may depend on the current state. For each state–action pair, there is a probability distribution that represents the likelihood of transitioning to different states after taking a particular action. Also associated with each state–action pair is a numerical reward or cost that quantifies the desirability or undesirability of being in a particular state and taking a specific action. The goal of a MDP is to find a *policy*, a mapping from states to actions, that maximizes the expected long-term reward or minimizes the expected long-term cost that accrues to an agent.

Q-learning uses a value function called a *Q-function* to estimate the expected cumulative reward for taking a particular action in a given state. The Q-learning algorithm follows the *Bellman equation* (1957), which states that the optimal Q-value for a state–action pair is equal to the immediate reward obtained from that action plus the discounted maximum Q-value of the next state. The Q-function, typically denoted as $Q(s, a)$, represents the expected cumulative reward when the agent takes action a in state s and follows the optimal policy thereafter. The goal of Q-learning is to iteratively update the Q-values until they converge to their optimal values. Because Q-learning often requires maintaining and updating a value table or function for every state–action pair, it can be more computationally demanding for larger state or action spaces.

An important aspect of Q-learning is that it balances exploration and exploitation by using an exploration strategy to occasionally select random actions and learn about their rewards. Over time, the agent gradually shifts its focus toward exploiting optimal actions, i.e., those that have delivered higher rewards. We formally describe the Q-learning algorithm in Table 4.1.

The Q-learning algorithm starts with initializing the Q-values for all state–action pairs and then interacts with the environment. At each step, the agent selects an action based on a decision strategy that balances exploration and exploitation. It receives a reward (positive or negative) and observes the next state. The Q-values are updated based on the observed reward and the maximum Q-value of the next state. The agent continues this process of interacting and updating Q-values until it converges to the optimal Q-values,

Table 4.1. Q-learning algorithm.

$Q(s, a) = R(s, a) + \gamma * \max\left(Q(s', a')\right),$

where

$Q(s, a)$ is the Q-value for state s and action a.

$R(s, a)$ is the immediate reward obtained for taking action a in state s.

γ is the discount factor that determines the importance of future rewards compared to immediate rewards. It is a value between 0 and 1.

s' is the next state that the agent transitions to after taking action a in state s.

a' is the next action the agent selects in state s.

The Q-learning algorithm iteratively updates Q-values based on rewards experienced during exploration. The updates are performed using the following update rule:

$Q(s, a) = (1 - \alpha) \times Q(s, a) + \alpha \times (R(s, a) + \gamma \times \max Q(s', a')),$

where

α is the learning rate that determines the weight given to the new information compared to the existing Q-value. It is a value between 0 and 1.

---

which represent the best action choices for each state. Over time, the learned Q-values can then be used to determine the optimal policy that the agent uses to guide his/her actions. We note that our implementation of Q-learning utilizes the UCB algorithm. Unless otherwise noted, we randomly vary the learning rate α and the exploration rate in each iteration of our simulations.

Now that we have reviewed the fundamental mathematics of the Q-learning algorithm, let us apply it to a set of more complex games that have wide applicability to geopolitical analysis.

4.3 The War of Attrition

The first game that we describe is the *War of Attrition* (WA). This game is a mathematical model of direct conflict between two players.

It is thus a game that has wide applicability to a number of scenarios in international affairs. The WA game is also typically formulated as a sequential game. In the game, each player independently decides when to retreat from a conflict. Each player has a cost C associated with remaining in the conflict, and an object with value V that they seek to obtain by staying in the conflict. The goal of the players in the WA game is to find the optimal balance between the potential gain from staying in the conflict and the cost associated with prolonging it. The game is played over a finite number of rounds. As the game is played through multiple iterations, players update their strategies based on their observed payoffs. The players' aim is to converge toward a Nash equilibrium, where neither player has an incentive to deviate from their chosen actions given the actions of their opponent(s). In Table 4.2, we show the basic payoff structure of the game.

In the matrix in Table 4.2, V_i represents the value or benefit that each player receives from staying in the conflict while C_i represents the cost incurred by each player for staying in the conflict. There are four action combinations. In the action combination in the upper left of the matrix, both players decide to stay in the conflict and receive their respective object values minus their respective costs. In the upper-right corner of the matrix, Player 1 fights, while Player 2 decides to give up. Player 1 receives object value V_1 minus cost C_1 and Player 2 incurs C_2. In the lower-left corner of the matrix, Player 1 gives up, while Player 2 fights. Player 1 incurs cost C_1 and Player 2 receives object value V_2 minus cost C_2. In the lower-right corner of the matrix, both players give up and receive a payoff of $-C_i$.

Aside from actual military engagements, the WA can be used to model many types of geopolitical interactions, such as the occasionally competitive monetary policies implemented by central banks.

Table 4.2. War of Attrition Game.

		Player 2 Continue Fighting	Player 2 Give Up
Player 1	Continue Fighting	V_1–C_1, V_2–C_2	V_1–C_1, –C_2
	Give Up	–C_2, V_2–C_2	–C_1, –C_2

For example, in the "race to the bottom" scenario that the global economy experienced following the Great Financial Crisis (GFC), central banks were perceived as competing with each other in a race to stimulate economic growth in their respective countries. In order to do so, they each maintained an easy, low-interest-rate policy over many periods. The exact mechanics of how they did so are not important (e.g., discount rate, QE) as the risk that any central bank undertakes in enacting an easy monetary policy is that, eventually, inflation rates may reach a level that threatens price stability. In the context of the WA, each central bank places a value V_i on economic growth that is achieved through their maintenance of an easy monetary policy and a respective cost C_i, which is the inflationary pressure (whether observed or expected) that is incurred by each bank in successive rounds. Eventually, a winner emerges when all the central banks, except one, "surrender" and stop easing. In the post-GFC easing war of attrition, the clear winner was Japan. Japan was able to maintain its easy monetary policy while other major economies, the US, EU, and the UK in particular, commenced with an extended period of interest rate hikes in order to combat inflation.

As in many actual cases of the WA, those involving central banks will likely involve different and evolving values for V and C for each bank. Let us examine the foregoing version of the WA in a simulation. However, rather than using singular values for V and C, we will modify the payoff structure in Table 4.2 so that each central bank has values and costs that fall in a particular range. We assume that in each round both values and costs are randomly chosen from the stated range. The payoffs can thus change through successive rounds. We show a numerical version of this modified payoff structure in Table 4.3, using the Fed and ECB as our players.

We now run a simulation in which each player uses Q-learning in order to determine the optimal strategy to use against the other bank.

Table 4.3. War of Attrition Game II.

		ECB	
		Maintain Easy Policy	Halt Easing
Fed	Maintain Easy Policy	$[2,6]-[2,5], [1,4]-[2,4]$	$[2,6]-[2,5], 0$
	Halt Easting	$0, [1,4]-[2,4]$	$0, 0$

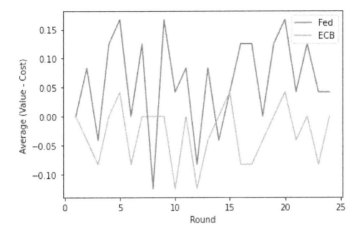

Figure 4.1. Average Net Payoff in Central Bank War of Attrition Game.

In Figure 4.1, we show the results of a simulation over twenty-four rounds and one thousand iterations, with each round representing some unit of time (e.g., months). The figure shows the average net payoff (Value–Cost) for each central bank over time. We see that, overall, given our respective inputs for growth and inflation for each central bank, the Fed is in a somewhat better position to withstand the risk of higher inflation because its detrimental effects are outweighed by the growth that an easy monetary policy potentially produces. We note, however, that the intent of the simulation is not to help us determine precisely *when* one of the players will give up but to determine *which* player is more likely to give up given the dynamics of the players' net payoffs over time.

4.4 Signaling Games

We next consider the *signaling game* introduced by Michael Spence (1973), which explores the dynamics of information transmission between two players, the *sender* and the *receiver*. The sender possesses private information about his/her own type, while the receiver does not have direct access to this information. The sender aims to strategically transmit a signal to the receiver to influence his/her behavior, as the information that the sender possesses is relevant to the receiver's decision-making process. For example, imagine a situation where a company is looking to hire employees, and there are different types of employees available. Each employee has a certain level of ability, which is unknown to the employers. The employees, however, have more accurate information about their own abilities than the employers do. In this game, the employees have two options: They can either choose to signal their ability to the company by taking an action that reveals information about themselves or they can choose not to signal and keep their information private. The employers, on the other hand, must decide whether or not to hire an employee based on the information they receive. However, signaling is not costless for the employees. Signaling costs will vary depending on their type (i.e., level of ability). The cost of signaling is lower for employees with higher ability and higher for those with lower ability. In this example, education acts as a costly signal that higher-ability individuals are more likely to invest in and successfully complete. The employers, being aware of this cost structure, understand that a signal from an employee with a higher ability level is more credible because it is relatively cheaper to provide. They can then use this information to make more informed hiring decisions.

Signaling is an important aspect of many types of interactions between political and economic institutions, including monetary policy. Signaling helps central banks convey their policy intentions and objectives to the public. Clear and transparent communication is essential to providing guidance on a central bank's goals, such as price stability, maximum employment, and/or ensuring financial stability. By effectively signaling their intentions via forward guidance and public assessments of economic conditions, inflation, and potential policy responses, central banks can influence market expectations and shape economic behavior in their desired manner.

We can formulate a monetary policy version of the signaling game in which the sender represents a central bank and the receiver represents the market. We imagine a scenario where the central bank has embarked on a program to fight inflation. The central bank has multiple types, each associated with a different monetary policy action. The market, on the other hand, receives benefits when it correctly identifies the type of the central bank based on the signal it receives. To the original version of the game, we also add a "signal quality" parameter that gauges the clarity with which the central bank coveys its policies. We posit three types for the central bank,

Slightly Hawkish, Hawkish, and Very Hawkish. We denote the types by $\theta \in \{\theta_1, \theta_2, \ldots, \theta_n\}$, where θ is the true type of the central bank. We denote the signals sent by the bank by $s \in \{s_1, s_2, \ldots, s_n\}$, where s is the actual signal sent by the bank. The signals can be specific policy pronouncements or more general statements and commentary.

In our version of the game, the costs associated with signaling for each type represent the estimated value of the inflation rate that is likely to materialize when the central bank takes a particular monetary policy action. The payoff received by the market represents varying degrees of expected equity returns that market participants will enjoy as a result of making better investment decisions when they correctly identify the type of the central bank based on the signal they receive. However, if receivers misinterpret the signals provided by the sender, they will face a penalty in the form of a negative investment return. As mentioned, we also posit a signal quality parameter that affects the market's (i.e., receiver's) decision-making. A lower signal quality value reduces the chances of the receiver making the right decision. The net payoff for the receiver is calculated as the raw payoff minus the applicable penalty.

With our model description in place, we are now in a position to run our simulation. We run the simulation over twenty rounds and one thousand iterations. As stated, we assume that the central bank has three types — Slightly Hawkish, Hawkish, and Very Hawkish. We also initially assume that the central bank is able to send three different signals. Again, signals are specific statements that the central bank uses to convey its policy intentions. Of course, in actuality, there may be more than three statements that are used to this effect. The ability of a central bank to express its policies clearly varies depending on the particular central bank personnel delivering the messages, typically the chairman and other senior bank officials. Our signal quality parameter can take on values in the range 0 to 1. In our initial simulation, we assume that the signal quality value is 0.8. After running our initial simulation, we will run a second simulation where we assume a lower value for the signal quality parameter.

For the costs associated with each central bank type, we assume that the inflation rates are 5%, 6%, and 7% for the Slightly Hawkish, Hawkish, and Very Hawkish types, respectively. The equity returns (payoffs) associated with correctly identifying the central bank type are 2%, 7%, and 12% for the Slightly Hawkish, Hawkish, and Very

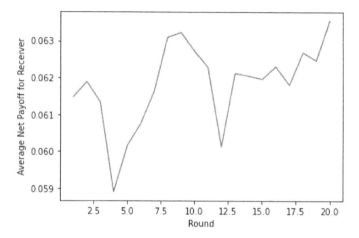

Figure 4.2. Average Net Payoff in Central Bank Signaling Game.

Hawkish types, respectively. The penalties that are imposed on the market for misreading central bank signals are 6%, 5%, and 10%, respectively, for the Slightly Hawkish, Hawkish, and Very Hawkish types. These penalties are applied to the market and subtracted from the cumulative equity returns up to a given point in time.

With our input parameters specified, we proceed to show the results of our initial simulation. In Figure 4.2, we see that while the net payoff (benefits–penalties) fluctuates, it is tightly range-bound. This is in part a result of a high signal quality value, which allows the receiver to avoid frequent misinterpretations of the sender's signal. We also see that overall, the market learns to make better decisions as the rounds progress.

Now let us examine a case where the signal quality is significantly weaker, with a value of 0.2. In Figure 4.3, we see that with the weaker level of signal quality, the net payoff (benefits–penalties) is still tightly range-bound but less so than in the previous example. More importantly, the level of the net payoffs is markedly lower than that produced in the previous simulation. This is not a surprise as with a lower signal quality, signals are more prone to misinterpretation and hence driving poorer decisions. We can also observe that there does not seem to be as much learning as the rounds progress. This is also not a surprise as it is difficult to learn when the information an agent is supposed to learn from is less reliable. One question

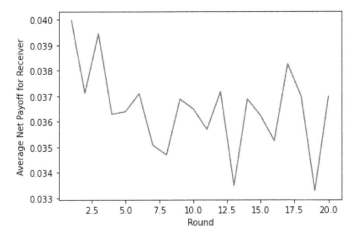

Figure 4.3. Average Net Payoff in Central Bank Signaling Game.

regarding signal quality pertains to what the source of the signal quality value is. Of course, it is possible to simply posit a value based on one's subjective views. But more objective approaches are also available. For example, one can review a major expression of policy, e.g., FOMC statements, count the pairs of inconsistent statements, and use the formula $1 - \frac{n}{10}$ to derive the value for the signal quality parameter, where n is the number of inconsistent statements identified.

4.5 Stackelberg Games

The next game that we consider is the *Stackelberg game*, a sequential game where players make decisions in a specific order.[2] One of the players is the leader and the other is the follower. The leader moves first and commits to a strategy before the follower chooses a strategy. In the Stackelberg game, the leader has a strategic advantage by moving first and by having the ability to observe the follower's actions before making a decision. This allows the leader to anticipate the follower's response and strategically choose an action to maximize his/her own payoff.

---

[2] For additional insight on Stackelberg games, see Stackelberg (1934, 2011), Simaan and Cruz (1973), Conitzer and Sandholm (2006), and Li and Sethi (2017).

The Stackelberg game is commonly used to model situations where one player has more power or influence than the other. This structure is ever present in geopolitics, where countries, institutions, and individuals often have significant leverage over one another. The relationship between central banks is a case in point. The central banks of larger and/or more developed countries will typically act as the policy leaders for the central banks of countries or regions that are relatively less influential in the international system. For example, we could assume that the Fed is the leader in a game with the ECB. In this case, the Fed would first set the federal funds rate in the United States and the ECB would follow by setting the main refinancing rate in the Eurozone.

In a Stackelberg game, the leader aims to find the optimal strategy that maximizes payoff, considering the follower's best response. The follower, on the other hand, aims to find the best response to the leader's action that maximizes his/her own payoff. The solution concept in a Stackelberg game is the Stackelberg equilibrium. It is a pair of strategies, where the leader's strategy maximizes payoff given the follower's best response to the leader's action. This equilibrium captures the idea that the leader's action is observed by the follower, who then responds optimally, resulting in a stable outcome.

The beliefs of the players can be important in Stackelberg games. For example, the Fed may have beliefs about the ECB's reaction function, capturing how the ECB adjusts its interest rate based on the Fed's policy decisions. The Fed may also have beliefs about economic conditions and their impact on the effectiveness of its policy decisions. The ECB may in turn have beliefs about the Fed's reaction function, capturing how the Fed adjusts its interest rate based on the ECB's policy decisions. The ECB may also have its own beliefs about global economic conditions and their impact on the effectiveness of *its* policy decisions.

Let us illustrate this interaction between the two central banks in a simulation. We assume that the Fed has the twin goals of controlling inflation and maximizing employment. We assume that the ECB only has the goal of controlling inflation. As the leader, the Fed acts first, setting the interest rate, and the ECB observes the Fed's decision and then adjusts its own interest rate accordingly. The Stackelberg equilibrium is reached when the Fed chooses its optimal strategy to maximize its payoff, considering the best response of the ECB.

Similarly, the ECB chooses its best response strategy given the Fed's chosen strategy. The payoff for each central bank is a function of the interest rate decisions of both the Fed and the ECB and captures the trade-off between controlling inflation and maximizing employment.

Formally, we say that at any point in time, the Fed chooses an optimal action a_f to maximize its payoff Π_{Fed}. The Fed's optimal action is determined by solving

$$\max_{a_f} \Pi_{\text{Fed}}(a_f, a_e^*(a_f)), \quad (4.1)$$

where a_e^* represents the ECB's response to the Fed's chosen action. The ECB's optimal action is determined in an analogous manner. After observing the Fed's action a_f, the ECB must determine its best response a_e in order to maximize its own payoff Π_{ECB}.

The payoffs for each central bank are derived as follows:

$$\Pi_{\text{Fed}} = -\alpha_1^{\text{Fed}} \left(\text{action}_{a_f} - \pi_{\text{target}}^{\text{Fed}} \right)^2 - \alpha_2^{\text{Fed}} \left(\text{action}_{a_f} - y_{\text{target}}^{\text{Fed}} \right)^2$$
$$\quad - \delta_1^{\text{Fed}} \left(\text{action}_{a_f} - \pi_{\text{target}}^{\text{ECB}} \right).$$

$$\Pi_{\text{ECB}} = -\beta_1^{\text{ECB}} \left(\text{actions}_{a_e} - \pi_{\text{target}}^{\text{ECB}} \right)^2 - \delta_1^{\text{ECB}} \left(\text{action}_{a_e} - \pi_{\text{target}}^{\text{Fed}} \right).$$
$$(4.2)$$

The parameters α_1 and β_1 represent the importance assigned by the Fed and ECB, respectively, to achieving their inflation targets. The parameter α_2 represents the importance attached by the Fed to achieving its employment target. A higher value for a parameter indicates a higher weight or importance assigned to the corresponding target, with a correspondingly larger impact on the payoffs for the players. These values are relative weights and are not restricted to any particular range.

Each bank takes monetary policy actions which we, for simplicity, assume are randomly drawn at the start of each round of play. As we see in (4.2), payoffs are a function of a bank's ability to match its target as well as coordinate with the other bank. To the latter end, we posit δ parameters that represent "coordination penalties" specific to each central bank. They represent the negative effect imposed on each central bank based on the deviation of their actions from those of the other central bank. If the inflation produced by the

ECB's action exceeds that produced by the Fed, a positive δ_1^{ECB} value will amplify the negative impact on the ECB's payoff. The penalty thus indicates a desire for some level of coordination or alignment between their policies. The solution to the optimization problems will yield the optimal interest rate decisions for the Fed and ECB in the Stackelberg equilibrium, considering their respective objectives and actions.

With the formal description of the players' decision-making process in place, we now proceed to show the results of a multi-round simulation of the game. As mentioned, we assume that the Fed and ECB each have independent inflation and employment targets. They are also assumed to have a desire to coordinate their actions. In Figure 4.4, we show the inputs and the evolution of average output

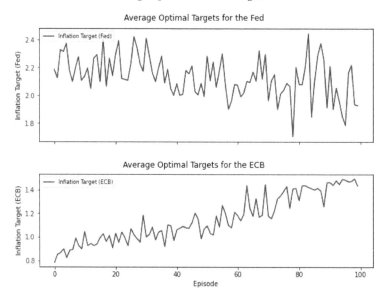

Figure 4.4. Stackelberg Game Inputs and Results for the Fed and ECB.

targets for each central bank over one hundred rounds and one thousand iterations.

In Figure 4.4, we see that in the case of both central banks, the optimal targets respond to their asymmetric payoff functions. Specifically, we see that because δ_{Fed} is 1.5 compared to the δ_{ECB} of 0.5, there is more effort to coordinate on the part of the Fed. Indeed, we see that the Fed's optimal inflation target trends lower over time as it tries to come closer to the ECB's. The optimal inflation target for the ECB, on the other hand, gets progressively higher as it approaches and eventually achieves its stated target of 1.5%. We note that this example represents a relatively simple model setup. The model inputs and payoffs can of course be further refined to reflect more complex relationships between central banks.

In terms of practical applications, a Stackelberg game such as the one presented here can help us hone in on a range of possible inflation rates for a given country as a function of its monetary policy, given our confidence in banks' propensity to coordinate and our stipulated payoff functions for each bank. In particular, by varying the values of the inputs, a type of "sensitivity analysis" can be developed whereby we gain an understanding of the range of inflation outcomes for different central banks based on different combinations of input values.

4.6 Pursuit–Evasion Games

Next, we analyze *Pursuit–Evasion games*. These games are mathematical models that capture the dynamics of pursuit and evasion between two players.[3] They are commonly applied to military operations, robotics, and law enforcement. In Pursuit–Evasion games, the Pursuer aims to make contact with the Evader, while the Evader tries to avoid contact with the Pursuer for as long as possible. Both the Pursuer and the Evader are assumed to have their own objectives and strategies.

Pursuit–Evasion games can be described mathematically using differential equations. In basic Pursuit–Evasion games, we have two players: the Pursuer P and the Evader E, both of which have their

---

[3]The classis works on Pursuit–Evasion games include Isaacs (1965) and Petrosyan (1993).

respective positions and velocities. We denote the position of the Pursuer at time t as $P(t)$ and the position of the Evader as $E(t)$. Their respective velocities are denoted by $V_p(t)$ and $V_e(t)$. The dynamics of the Pursuit–Evasion game can be represented by the following set of equations:

$$\frac{dP(t)}{dt} = V_p(t). \tag{4.3}$$

$$\frac{dE(t)}{dt} = V_e(t). \tag{4.4}$$

The dynamics of the game are determined by the movement rules and constraints of the Pursuer and Evader. These rules specify how their states change over time based on their actions and the current state of the game. The specific dynamics can vary depending on the scenario and the specific models used. Analyzing a Pursuit–Evasion game involves studying the strategies and optimal actions for both the Pursuer and Evader. The objective is generally to find a strategy that leads to an equilibrium, where neither player has an incentive to change his action given the action of the other player.

The Pursuit–Evasion game is characterized by the relative motion between the Pursuer and Evader. The objective of the Pursuer is to catch (or intercept) the Evader, while the Evader aims to avoid capture. The specific evasion strategy can vary depending on the scenario and the Evader's objectives. It can involve changing direction, speed, or both, to create separation from the Pursuer. One commonly used pursuit strategy is called "proportional navigation," where the Pursuer adjusts its velocity based on the line-of-sight (LOS) rate. The LOS rate is the derivative of the angle between the Pursuer's velocity vector and the vector connecting the Pursuer and Evader positions. The velocity vector $V(t)$ for a player can be derived as follows:

$$V(t) = K * L\dot{O}S(t) * L\hat{O}S(t), \tag{4.5}$$

where $L\dot{O}S(t)$ represents the derivative (rate) of the line of sight at time t, $L\hat{O}S(t)$ represents the unit vector of the line of sight at time t, and K is a scalar constant.

A well-known Pursuit-Evasion game is the *Homicidal Chauffeur*. The game involves two players: the Homicidal Chauffeur and the Victim. The Homicidal Chauffeur has two options, either drive straight or swerve, while the Victim can choose to either stay in his current position or jump out of the way. As in many other games, each player's goal is to maximize their payoff. The players make their decisions without knowing what the other player will choose. This lack of information adds an element of inherent uncertainty to the game.

It is important to note that the Homicidal Chauffeur game differs from standard Pursuit–Evasion games in a few key respects. First, the Victim's goal is to avoid capture rather than evade the Chauffeur indefinitely. Once the Victim reaches his destination, the game ends regardless of whether the Chauffeur is close or not. Second, the Chauffeur follows a predefined path that he may or may not deviate from. The Victim's challenge is to anticipate the Chauffeur's actions. In traditional Pursuit–Evasion games, both the Pursuer and the Evader have more active roles. The Evader typically aims to evade the Pursuer indefinitely, and both players make decisions based on the current state of the game. Thus, the dynamics of the Pursuit–Evasion game are often more complex. Finally, in the Homicidal Chauffeur game, the Chauffeur's objective is to reach the Victim and *inflict harm* upon the Victim after capturing him. This contrasts with traditional Pursuit–Evasion games, where inflicting harm on the Evader is not a standard feature of the interaction between players.

In the following simulation, we present a hybrid type of game where the notion of "harm" from the Homicidal Chauffeur is utilized within a framework that includes the more complex dynamics of typical Pursuit–Evasion games. We believe this type of hybrid game can be used to model many situations in international affairs such as trade negotiations. Accordingly, in our example, we assume that two countries are engaged in a "trade war" where one country, the Pursuer, is attempting to catch up to the export volumes of another country, the Evader. We assume that each country has four actions available to it: (1) reduce tariffs, (2) weaken currency, (3) export subsidies, or (4) export tax rebates. For each country, each action has a different *speed*. The speed variable in the present context can be interpreted as a gauge of the effectiveness of a given policy action. Thus, certain actions are more likely to reduce the gap between Pursuer and Evader, something that the players will learn over time. Each action speed is posited as a real-valued number with random noise.

We assume that there are ten states in the game, each representing the level of respective market access that each country has, based on the actions they have taken. We also model our game as a Bayesian game. To that end, we assume that the Pursuer has prior probabilities with regard to which state the game is in. For simplicity, we assume that the Pursuer views each state as equiprobable (i.e., each state has a prior of 10%).[4] For the payoffs, we assume that the Pursuer gains a reward of 100 for capturing the Evader in a given round and a reward of $10 - d$ for not capturing the Evader, where d represents the distance between the two countries.

In Figure 4.5, we show the results of the above-described simulation. For this simulation, the speeds that are assumed for each player and action are as follows:

Pursuer: [reduce tariffs: 1.6, weaken currency: 1.8, export subsidies: 1.4, export tax rebates: 1.2].

Evader: [reduce tariffs: 1.5, weaken currency: 1.7, export subsidies: 1.6, export tax rebates: 1.3].

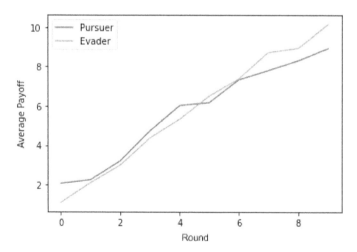

Figure 4.5. Homicidal Chauffeur Trade War Simulation Results.

---

[4]It is of course possible to have "informative priors" and thereby express more precise information about each state.

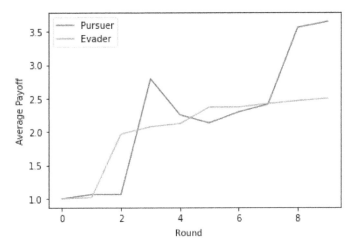

Figure 4.6. Homicidal Chauffeur Trade War Simulation Results II.

As we see in Figure 4.5, the trade war between the Pursuer and Evader countries is a closely contested battle until round seven, at which point the Evader seems to learn from prior rounds and breaks away from the Pursuer country. This would be akin to one country coming to learn the best policy responses to another over time as prior policies take effect and their respective effectiveness becomes evident.

Now, let us take a look at the same simulation but with a slight adjustment to the speed of one of the Pursuer's actions. In particular, we increase the Pursuer's speed for the "reduce tariffs" action to 1.8 from 1.6 in our initial simulation. In this case, this is clearly advantageous to the Pursuer in relation to the Evader. We leave all the other speeds as before. In Figure 4.6, we show the results of this modified simulation. We see that the Pursuer country eventually overtakes the Evader country and that this only happens after a number of rounds, presumably after the Pursuer has learned which policies (actions) are most effective, namely, the "reduce tariffs" policy.

4.7 Games with Lexicographic Beliefs

In this book, we have placed special focus on games of incomplete information, which indicates the importance of epistemic considerations in strategic interaction. *Games with lexicographic beliefs* are another class of games involving player beliefs. These games model a player who believes that his opponent will behave in a certain order of preference or priority.[5]

Let us consider a game where Country A and Country B are involved in negotiations regarding rights to a natural resource in a disputed territory. An example would be natural gas extraction in coastal waters that are adjacent to both countries. We assume that Country A has lexicographic beliefs about the behavior of Country B based on Country B's past behavior and the public pronouncements of public officials in that country. Now, suppose that Country A believes that Country B has three possible actions, ranked in the following lexicographic order of preference:

Action 1: Negotiate for Shared Use of Natural Resource.
Action 2: Unilateral Exploitation of Natural Resource.
Action 3: Military Action to Occupy Territory where Natural Resource is Located.

We further assume that Country A assigns probabilities to these strategies according to its beliefs about Country B's preferences. Country A believes that Country B will choose Action 1 with a probability of 0.6, Action 2 with a probability of 0.3, and Action 3 with a probability of 0.1. We also posit a payoff matrix for each possible action. We show this in Table 4.4.

Table 4.4. Payoff Matrix for Game with Lexicographic Beliefs.

		Country B		
		Action 1	Action 2	Action 3
Country A	Action 1	3, 2	1, 3	4, 5
	Action 2	2, 4	2, 3	3, 1
	Action 3	1, 3	4, 1	2, 2

---

[5]For more on lexicographic games, see Perea (2012).

Now we are in a position to calculate expected payoffs for Country A given each action choice:

Action 1 = (0.6 × 3) + (0.3 × 1) + (0.1 × 4) = 2.5.
Action 2 = (0.6 × 2) + (0.3 × 2) + (0.1 × 3) = 2.1.
Action 3 = (0.6 × 1) + (0.3 × 4) + (0.1 × 2) = 2.0.

Thus, given Country A's beliefs, we see that Action 1 has the highest expected payoff (2.5), so it is the optimal action for Country A to take. It is clear from Country A's belief structure that it does not believe that Country B is inclined toward aggressive actions (2 or 3). In our simulation below, we will assume that the probabilities posited in this single-round example are Country A's initial beliefs that evolve over time as it learns through experience. For Country B's beliefs, we assume that it initially believes that Country A will choose Action 1 with a probability of 0.3, Action 2 with a probability of 0.2, and Action 3 with a probability of 0.5. When we combine these probability values with Country B's payoffs from Table 4.4, we get the following expected payoffs for Country B:

Action 1 = (0.3 × 2) + (0.2 × 4) + (0.5 × 3) = 2.9.
Action 2 = (0.3 × 3) + (0.2 × 3) + (0.5 × 1) = 2.0.
Action 3 = (0.3 × 5) + (0.2 × 1) + (0.5 × 2) = 2.7.

As we see from our calculations, for Country B, Action 1 also has the highest expected payoff. So, after a single round, negotiation would be preferred by both countries. Now, we proceed to set up a multi-round simulation of the game using Q-learning. We utilize the same payoff matrix that we used in our initial example. The simulation runs for fifty rounds and is iterated over one thousand simulations. The exploration rates and learning rates for both countries are set to 0.1.

Once the simulation terminates, we see (Figure 4.7) that Country A ends up better off over the long run. This result is interesting because although Action 1 is the action with the highest expected payoff for both countries, its almost continual "exploitation" on the part of Country B leads to a significantly lower average payoff over time compared to Country A given Action 1's respective payoffs for each country (3 for country A, 2 for country B (Table 4.4)). However,

92   *Computational Global Macro*

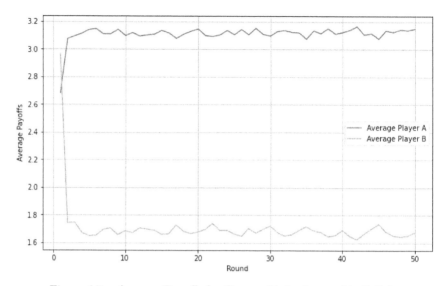

Figure 4.7.   Average Payoffs for Game with Lexicographic Beliefs.

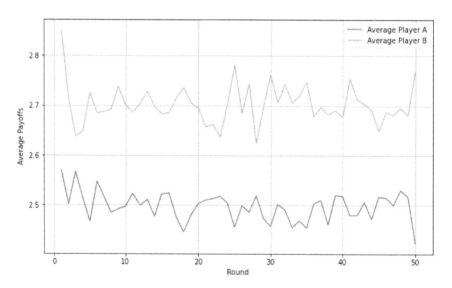

Figure 4.8.   Average Payoffs for Game with Lexicographic Beliefs II.

if the exploration rate for Country B is adjusted upward to 0.7, we get the output in Figure 4.8. As we can see, exploration works in Country B's favor and against Country A as most action combinations apart from (Action 1, Action 1) actually provide higher relative payoffs to Country B. Thus, we see that the utility of exploration is that it can help agents learn potentially beneficial actions that may not coincide with their initial views on the most beneficial action(s).

4.8 Concluding Points

In this chapter, we introduced Q-learning, a reinforcement learning algorithm that differs from CMABs in a number of respects, namely, that it is somewhat more adept at treating the temporal dynamics of agent interaction and that it gives agents the ability to influence future states by their present actions. While being able to more precisely model agent interaction over time is a critical aspect of analyzing international affairs, so is consideration of the causal drivers of geopolitical events. To that end, in Chapter 5, we will survey and discuss a wide spectrum of formal models of causal inference and analysis and also show how they can be combined with game theory and reinforcement learning to model geopolitical interaction.

References

Bellman, R.E. 1957. *Dynamic Programming*. Princeton, NJ: Princeton University Press.

Conitzer, V. and Sandholm, T. 2006. Computing the optimal strategy to commit to. *Proceedings of the 7th ACM Conference on Electronic Commerce (EC '06)*. Association for Computing Machinery, New York, NY, USA, 82–90.

Ha, D. and Schmidhuber, J. 2018. Recurrent experience replay in distributed reinforcement learning. *Proceedings of the 35th International Conference on Machine Learning (ICML-18)*, 1955–1964.

Hasselt, H.V. 2010. Double Q-learning. *Advances in Neural Information Processing Systems (NeurIPS)* 23: 2613–2621.

Hasselt, H.V., Guez, A., and Silver, D. 2016. Deep reinforcement learning with double Q-learning. In *AAAI Conference on Artificial Intelligence (AAAI)*, 2094–2010.

Isaacs, R. 1965. *Differential Games: A Mathematical Theory with Applications to Warfare and Pursuit, Control and Optimization.* New York: John Wiley & Sons.

Li, T. and Sethi, S.P. 2017. A review of dynamic stackelberg game models. *Discrete and Continuous Dynamical Systems — B* 22(1): 125–159.

Perea, A. 2012. *Epistemic Game Theory: Reasoning and Choice.* Cambridge: Cambridge University Press.

Petrosyan, L. 1993. *Differential Games of Pursuit (Series on Optimization, Vol 2).* Singapore: World Scientific.

Schulman, J., Levine, S., Abbeel, P., Jordan, M. and Moritz, P. 2015. Trust region policy optimization. *Proceedings of the 32nd International Conference on Machine Learning (ICML-15)*, 1889–1897.

Simaan, M., and Cruz, J.B. 1973. On the stackelberg strategy in nonzero-sum games. *Journal of Optimization Theory and Applications* 11(5): 533–555.

Spence, M. 1973. Job market signaling. *The Quarterly Journal of Economics* 87(3): 355–374.

Tesauro, G. 1995. Temporal Difference Learning and TD-Gammon. *Communications of the ACM* 38(3): 58–68.

von Stackelberg, H. 1934, 2011. *Market Structure and Equilibrium*, translated by Damien Bazin, Lynn Urch, and Rowland Hill, Berlin, and Heidelberg: Springer-Verlag.

Wang, Z., Schaul, T., Hessel, M., Hasselt, H. V., Lanctot, M. and de Freitas, N. 2016. Dueling network architectures for deep reinforcement learning. *Proceedings of the 33rd International Conference on Machine Learning (ICML-16)*, 1995–2003.

Watkins, C.J.C.H. and Dayan, P. 1992. Q-learning. *Machine Learning* 8(3–4): 279–292.

Chapter 5

Causal Inference in Models of Strategic Interaction

5.1 The Problem of Causality

Causal relations between actions, events, and processes have been objects of study for philosophers and scientists for centuries. Contemporary discussions of causality typically begin with the definition of causation provided by the philosopher David Hume (1777). Hume defines cause in the following manner:

$$C \text{ causes } E \equiv \text{Instantiations of } E \text{ regularly follow} \\ \text{instantiations of } C. \quad (5.1)$$

Hume's theory of causation is based on the observation of the "constant conjunction" of events and is thus a purely subjective one that assumes that human psychology is the source of the seeming necessity of causes leading to effects. Hume's definition of causation is empirically rooted and based on the observation that some events or actions seem to follow other actions and events more often than not. On the surface, Hume's definition of cause seems to leave open the possibility that C may be a cause of E even if E does not always follow C, i.e., C may not be a necessary condition for E. As such, subsequent definitions of cause have attempted to strengthen the definitional relationship between cause and effect in a number of ways. For example, a *counterfactual* definition of cause could be stated in the following manner:

$$C \text{ causes } E \equiv \text{If } C \text{ had not happened}, E \text{ would not have happened either.} \qquad (5.2)$$

Other definitions of cause have focused on particular aspects of the cause-and-effect relationship. For example, much of the causal language employed in economic policymaking seems to subscribe to the "manipulation" or "wiggle" conception of causality. The manipulation approach to causality is motivated in part by the causal inferences that are often made in a laboratory setting, where changes in one set of variables are observed after manipulating another set of variables.[1] Indeed, the idea of "no causation without manipulation" (Holland 1986) stems from the view that something should only be defined as a cause if it could be a treatment in an experiment. We may define this type of causality as follows:

$$C \text{ causes } E \equiv C \text{ causes } E \text{ if manipulating } C \text{ makes } E \text{ change.} \qquad (5.3)$$

The applicability of (5.3) is clearly seen in monetary policy where the federal funds rate is considered a variable that can be manipulated to produce changes in employment and inflation.[2] Application of the manipulation account is not limited to economic policy, however. Indeed, once we realize that all economic activity is the result of human intentionality and action, we realize that the manipulation account can be applied to most economic and market phenomena.[3]

---

[1] The manipulation account of causation is developed in Collingwood (1940), Gasking (1955), von Wright (1971), Menzies and Price (1993), and Woodward (2003). It has had significant influence on experimental design (Cook and Campbell, 1979) and artificial intelligence (Pearl, 2009).

[2] The federal funds rate could thus be considered a "common cause" to changes in growth and inflation.

[3] The anthropocentric orientation of the manipulative account has been criticized by some because it does not seem to admit non-human drivers of causality (Hausman, 1986, 1998). However, the criticism seems *prima facie* impotent for most accounts of causality in the social sciences, including economics. That said, we recognize that not *all* economically relevant causal relations are due to human manipulation. For example, different weather patterns can cause changes in crop yields. However, while those changes are not a result of human manipulation, the changes in commodity prices that follow are.

The manipulation account is consistent with another popular approach to causal modeling, the *probabilistic causation* account. In the following, we lay out the basic formulas of probabilistic causality using a well-known framework developed by Suppes (1970).[4] We define a *positive cause* in the following manner:

$$t < t'. \tag{5.4}$$

$$P(C_t) > 0. \tag{5.5}$$

$$P(E_{t'}|C_t) > P(E_{t'}). \tag{5.6}$$

The definitions state that (1) causes must precede effects; (2) the probability of a cause is greater than zero; and (3) the probability of an effect given a cause is greater than the probability of the effect by itself. We define a *negative cause* in an analogous fashion:

$$t < t'. \tag{5.7}$$

$$P(C_t) > 0. \tag{5.8}$$

$$P(E_{t'}|C_t) < P(E_{t'}). \tag{5.9}$$

The probabilistic approach to causality may be combined with the manipulation account to produce the following definition:

$$C \text{ causes } E \equiv C \text{ causes } E \text{ if manipulating } C \text{ raises}$$
$$\text{the probability that } E \text{ will change.} \tag{5.10}$$

Whatever underlying conceptual framework one subscribes to, there are two basic uses of any causal model. The first is to accurately model and apply available causal knowledge and the second is to discover or infer hitherto unknown causal relations. That said, developing a framework for representing and/or understanding causal relations between economic entities is arguably more challenging than doing so in the natural sciences given the open nature of economic systems, which makes them generally inaccessible to the type of experimental analysis we find in other scientific domains.[5] As open systems, there are a multitude of potential common causes that

---

[4]Good (1961) provided an earlier account of probabilistic causation.
[5]This point has been previously discussed in Simonian et al. (2018).

may bring about a certain economic effect. Moreover, as noted by Hicks (1979), economics is characterized by a lack of "natural constants," timeless facts which can be discovered and measured. This is unlike physics, for example, which presupposes the existence of the latter kind of phenomena. Furthermore, in nature cause and effect are often observed to occur in (more or less) immediate succession. In contrast, economic phenomena frequently exhibit significant lags between observed causes and effects.

Despite its epistemic opacity, economic causality has nevertheless been subject to a considerable degree of theorizing. Perhaps the most well-known characterization of economic causality is that provided by Granger (1969), who stated that for a given predictor x and target variable y, x causes y if

$$x \text{ temporally precedes } y, \tag{5.11}$$

$$x \text{ provides more predictively useful information than}$$
$$\text{a rival "naïve" predictor.} \tag{5.12}$$

One way of formally expressing (5.12) is $P(Y_{t+1}|X_t, Y_t) > P(Y_{t+1}|Y_t)$, which can be interpreted as saying that given a target variable Y, the probability of predicting its one-step-ahead value Y_{t+1} is higher given temporally prior information about a predictor variable X in addition to temporally prior information about Y alone. Granger causality may also be articulated in a more general form:

$$C \text{ causes } E \equiv C \text{ causes } E \text{ if there is information}$$
$$\text{transmission from } C \text{ to } E. \tag{5.13}$$

Granger's approach to causality is of course but one approach to economic causality. In Table 5.1, we show a classification of economic causality provided by Hoover (2008). The first distinction Hoover makes is between structural and process approaches to economic causality. The latter categories can be respectively viewed as orientated toward explanation and prediction. Structural approaches to economic causality are primarily concerned with explaining and formally characterizing economic phenomena. The *a priori* structural approaches, such as those taken by the Cowles Commission, consider economic theory as the primary tool for identifying economic causes. Inferential structural approaches, on the other hand, such as

Table 5.1. Theories of Economic Causality.

	Structural	Process
A Priori	Cowles Commission; Koopmans (1953); Hood and Koopmans (1953)	Zellner (1979)
Inferential	Simon (1953); Hoover (1990, 2001); Favero and Hendry (1992); Angrist and Krueger (1999, 2001)	Granger (1969); Sims (1980)

Source: Hoover (2008).

the approach presented by Simon (1953), accept that empirical data can be used to identify economic causes.

In contrast to structural approaches, inferential approaches to economic causality are primarily concerned with uncovering economic processes that can aid in the production of accurate forecasts. The *a priori* process approach of Zellner views theory as a means to produce successful predictions and as a way to distinguish genuine economic laws from accidental regularities and false generalizations. In contrast, the inferential process approach, best exemplified by the concept of Granger causality discussed earlier, more or less dispenses with any supporting background theory and instead looks to data to provide insight into predictively useful causal associations. Of course, not all approaches to causality in economics fit neatly into Hoover's classification scheme. Hoover's scheme is nevertheless useful in providing a basic classification of frameworks for causal analysis in economics.

We note that inferential process approaches are arguably the closest in spirit to methodologies that are more heavily oriented toward prediction, such as financial data science (FDS).[6] This is also the case because FDS is inherently data oriented and less reliant on theory compared to traditional econometrics. Indeed, contrary to Zellner, it would seem that for FDS, "accidental regularities" will suffice as causal explanans as long as they help produce successful forecasts and have a sufficient history. Indeed, FDS also recognizes that informal "folk" theories and heuristics may at times provide valuable assistance in producing successful forecasts. Given this, FDS can be

---

[6]See Simonian and Fabozzi (2019) for an argument in support of this view.

considered a hybrid approach that does not fit neatly into one of the four boxes in Table 5.1, but is nevertheless most sympathetic to the inferential process approach.

5.2 Causal Inference

Causal inference is a branch of statistics that aims to understand the cause-and-effect relationships between variables. In particular, it is concerned with determining the causal effect of an intervention or treatment on an outcome of interest. In traditional statistical analysis, the estimation of associations or correlations between variables is the primary area of focus. However, associations by themselves do not necessarily imply causation. Causal inference goes beyond associations to investigate the relationships and underlying mechanisms of the factors that drive and influence observed outcomes. Methods of causal inference generally make use of observational data or experimental studies, such as randomized controlled trials (RCTs),[7] to identify and estimate causal effects. Various statistical techniques, such as regression modeling, propensity score matching,[8] instrumental variable analysis,[9] and difference-in-differences analysis,[10] are commonly used in causal inference.

---

[7] A randomized control trial (RCT) is a type of study where participants are randomly assigned into groups to receive different interventions or treatments. Outcomes between the groups are compared to help determine cause-and-effect relationships between the intervention and its outcomes.

[8] Propensity score matching is a statistical method that is used when an RCT is not available. It pairs individuals from treatment and control groups based on their likelihood (propensity) of receiving the treatment. It aims to create comparable groups, minimizing the influence of confounding variables and enabling more accurate comparisons of treatment effects in observational studies.

[9] Instrumental variable analysis is also used in the absence of the ability to conduct an RCT and involves the identification of an instrumental variable — a variable that is correlated with the treatment variable of interest, but only affects the outcome through its influence on the treatment.

[10] Difference-in-difference analysis involves analyzing the differences in outcomes before and after the treatment for both groups, allowing researchers to estimate the causal impact of the treatment by accounting for other factors that affect the outcome trends over time.

The basic process of causal inference is conducted in discrete steps. The first step involves the identification of causal variables, the variables that are potential predictors of the outcome of interest. This requires a clear understanding of the research question and the underlying theory and/or specific domain knowledge. The next step is establishing a causal relationship between the treatment or intervention and the outcome by considering other factors that may confound or influence the relationship. This involves addressing issues such as selection bias and engaging in counterfactual reasoning. Finally, the magnitude of causal effects needs to be estimated.

In the context of causal inference, there are three types of causal effects that are commonly discussed. The first is known as the *Average Treatment Effect* (ATE): The Average Treatment Effect measures the average difference in the outcome variable between two groups, where one group is exposed to a treatment or intervention and the other group is not. It quantifies the average change in the outcome that can be attributed to the treatment. The second type of causal effect is the *Conditional Average Treatment Effect* (CATE): The Conditional Average Treatment Effect measures the average difference in the outcome variable between two groups, considering specific conditions or subgroups. It focuses on the causal effect within a particular subgroup of the population, conditioning on specific variables or characteristics. The final type of causal effect is the *Individual Treatment Effect* (ITE): The Individual Treatment Effect refers to the specific causal effect for an individual unit or subject in a study. It captures the unique impact of the treatment on each individual separately, accounting for heterogeneity across individuals.

5.2.1 The do Operator

Closely related to the three types of causal effects mentioned in the previous section is the *do* operator (Pearl, 2009). The operator, which is denoted as "$do(X = x)$" or simply "$do(X)$," is a notation used in causal inference to represent interventions on a specific variable X in a causal model. The *do* operator allows us to explicitly specify that we are manipulating the value of X, regardless of the actual mechanisms that would determine its value. For example, with the ATE, we would have one group receiving the treatment, $do(X = 1)$, and another group not receiving the treatment, $do(X = 0)$. Here, the *do* operator would be used to enforce a specific treatment assignment (X = 1 or X = 0) in order to estimate and compare the average outcomes between treated and untreated groups. With the CATE, on the other hand, the *do* operator can be applied to different subgroups to estimate and compare the average outcomes for those specific groups. Finally, for the ITE, we would use the *do* operator to enforce specific treatment assignments (X = 1 or X = 0) for each individual unit, allowing us to observe and analyze the individual outcomes under different treatment scenarios.

The *do* operator thus helps us answer counterfactual, "what if" questions by simulating the effect of interventions on the variables in a model. Causal models are typically expressed visually using a directed acyclic graph (DAG). In a DAG, when we apply the *do* operator to a variable X, we are essentially assuming that X has been externally set to a specific value, independent of its observed causal relationships with other variables. This allows us to observe the counterfactual outcome of the system if X were to be changed, without actually changing the system itself. By using the *do* operator, we can observe and analyze causal effects and make predictions based on our hypothetical interventions, enabling us to estimate the impact of different interventions on various types of systems.

Causal inference and the application of the *do* operator are often implemented with the aid of a structural causal model (SCM), a type of causal model used to represent the causal relationships between variables in a system. SCMs consist of a DAG that represents the causal dependencies among variables, along with a set of structural equations that describe how each variable depends on its parent variables in the graph. SCMs are used to study the causal effects of interventions and to make predictions about the behavior of a system under different conditions. SCMs allow us to estimate the direct effects of interventions on the outcome variable while considering the dependencies and interactions between variables. SCMs also account for *confounding variables*, variables that influence both the dependent and independent variable(s), which can lead to spurious causal effect estimates. By including multiple interrelated variables, SCMs allow us to represent the causal structures of real-world systems more faithfully. In the context of SCMs, when we apply the *do* operator to an exogenous variable, we are effectively fixing the value of that variable to the specified *do* value for all observations in the dataset.

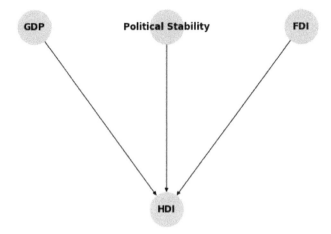

Figure 5.1. SCM Example 1.

This allows us to study the causal effect of the intervention on a particular variable while holding the other variables fixed.

Before we examine how the *do* operator works, let us first survey various types of SCMs. Consider the DAG in Figure 5.1.

The DAG[11] in Figure 5.1 is described by the following SCM:

$$\text{HDI} = \beta_{\text{GDP,HDI}} \cdot \text{GDP} + \beta_{\text{PS,HDI}} \cdot \text{PS} + \beta_{\text{FDI,HDI}} \cdot \text{FDI} + \varepsilon.$$

Or, consider the DAG in Figure 5.2, where one causal variable is a function of another.

The DAG in Figure 5.2 is represented by the following SCM:

$$B = \beta_{AB} \cdot A + \varepsilon_B,$$
$$C = \beta_{BC} \cdot B + \varepsilon_C,$$

where A = Expansionary Monetary Policy, B = Deposit Rates, and C = Bank Loans.

In any SCM model, we can include additional variables in the system of equations to account for confounding, such as the one shown in Figure 5.3. By controlling for confounding, the SCM approach provides more accurate and less biased causal effect estimates.

---

[11]This DAG describes the HDI (a country's Human Development Index value) as a function of a country's GDP (Gross Domestic Product), Political Stability, and FDI (Foreign Direct Investment).

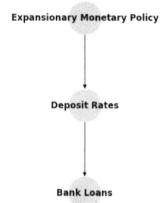

Figure 5.2. SCM Example 2.

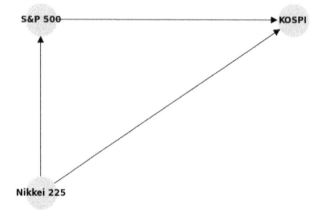

Figure 5.3. SCM with Confounder.

The SCM in Figure 5.3. can be described mathematically as follows:

$$S\&P\ 500 = \beta_{S\&P500,\ Nikkei\ 225} \cdot Nikkei\ 225 + \varepsilon_{S\&P\ 500}.$$

$$KOSPI = \beta_{KOSPI,S\&P500} \cdot S\&P500 + \beta_{KOSPI,Nikkei225}$$
$$\cdot Nikkei\ 225 + \varepsilon_{KOSPI}.$$

Now, let us walk through an example of an implementation of the *do* operator.

In the DAG in Figure 5.4, "Reduction in Interest Rates" causally influences both "Increased Consumer Spending" and "Increased

Causal Inference in Models of Strategic Interaction 105

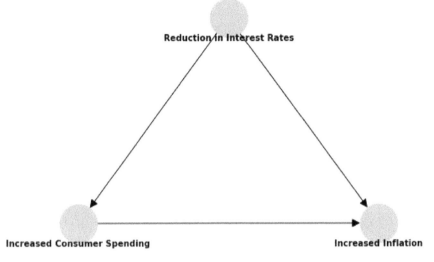

Figure 5.4. SCM with Confounder 2.

Inflation." The variable "Reduction in Interest Rates" is the confounding variable. To isolate the impact of "Increased Consumer Spending" on "Increased Inflation," we need to control for the confounding variable "Reduction in Interest Rates." This can be achieved by applying the *do*-operator to intervene on "Increased Consumer Spending" while accounting for the influence of "Reduction in Interest Rates." This means simulating an intervention by setting "Increased Consumer Spending" to a specific value independent of its usual causes and observing the effect on "Increased Inflation." To do this, we use what is known as the *backdoor adjustment*. The backdoor adjustment relies on the concept of conditioning on the paths to block the confounding effect. In estimating the causal effect of the treatment variable (A) on the outcome variable (C), we condition on the variables that are common causes to both (A) and (C) in the causal graph. This adjustment is known as "closing the backdoor paths." Thus, we examine the causal effect of setting A ("Increased Consumer Spending") =1 on C ("Increased Inflation" =1) without the influence of B ("Reduction in Interest Rates"). Formally, this is given by the following:

$$P(C = 1|do(A = 1)) = \Sigma P(C = 1|A = 1, \ B = b) \times P(B = b),$$

where the sum is taken over all possible values of B (b).

As an example, assume that
$$P(C = 1|A = 1, B = 0) = 0.2$$
and
$$P(C = 1|A = 1, B = 1) = 0.8$$
and further that
$$P(B = 0) = 0.6$$
$$P(B = 1) = 0.4$$
So we have
$$P(C = 1|do(A = 1)) = 0.2 \times 0.6 + 0.8 \times 0.4 = 0.44.$$

Thus, there is a 44% probability of increased inflation when consumer spending is increased, accounting for the influence of a reduction in interest rates.

5.3 Causal Reinforcement Learning

It is possible to explicitly apply causal concepts within reinforcement learning. There are several approaches that have been presented in the academic literature (e.g., Bareinboim *et al.* 2015, Lee and Bareinboim, 2019). Here, we will present a causal reinforcement learning model that will allow us to analyze strategic decision-making in the presence of unobserved causal drivers. This type of strategic analysis can be informative to macro investors, given the at times opaque nature of geopolitical events.

Consider a game with two players, specifically two countries engaged in trade negotiations. Each country must decide whether to cooperate or defect without knowing the other player's choice. However, in each round, there is not one possible game but two. The determinant of which game is played is an unobservable confounding variable which we call "Global Trade Conditions." This variable can take on one of two values: "Free Trade" or "Mercantilist." It is a confounder because it influences both the strategies (e.g., tit-for-tat) that players choose and the average payoffs accruing to each player, which are also influenced by the strategies that the players adopt.

In the Free Trade state, the game is the Battle of the Sexes game, where the players have an incentive to cooperate but differ on which mode of cooperation they prefer. In the Mercantilist state, the game is the Prisoner's Dilemma, where the incentive to cooperate may be weaker given the possibility of defection via tariffs or other trade barriers. As the game progresses through successive rounds, the players learn to adapt their strategies in the presence of this confounding influence.

The hidden variable pertaining to global trade conditions is generated using the Dirichlet distribution. It is employed to generate a probability distribution over the two possible states, "Free Trade" and "Mercantilist," for each round of the simulation. The Dirichlet distribution is well suited for modeling probabilities over multiple states since it generates random probability vectors that naturally satisfy the constraints of being within [0, 1] and summing to 1. The Dirichlet distribution takes a vector of parameters (*alpha*) as input, where each element of the vector represents a concentration parameter for the corresponding state of global trade conditions. The larger the value of alpha for a specific state, the more likely that state will be sampled. The Dirichlet distribution is useful because it allows us to create a wide range of probability distributions with different levels of uncertainty in a mathematically tractable manner.[12]

We now set up a simulation to analyze our game. We assume that Player 1 uses Q-learning to guide his actions. In contrast, we assume that Player 2 uses a reinforcement learning framework known as SARSA (State–Action–Reward–State–Action).[13] SARSA is an *on-policy learning algorithm*, meaning that it updates its Q-values based on the current policy that is being used for action selection. When updating the Q-value for a state–action pair (s, a), SARSA uses the next action (a') that is taken in the next state (s') using the current policy. Essentially, SARSA evaluates the value of the action

---

[12]The Dirichlet distribution is often used in Bayesian inference. For example, it can be used as a conjugate prior for the multinomial distribution. This means that when the likelihood function is a multinomial distribution and the prior distribution is a Dirichlet distribution, the posterior distribution, after observing data, is also a Dirichlet distribution.

[13]For more background on the SARSA algorithm, see Rummery and Niranjan (1994) and Sutton and Barto (1998).

that is actually chosen based on the current policy and updates the Q-values accordingly. In contrast to Q-learning, the SARSA update equation is as follows:

$$Q(s,a) \leftarrow Q(s,a) + \alpha[R + \gamma \times Q(s',a') - Q(s,a)], \qquad (5.14)$$

where $Q(s,a)$ represents the current estimated Q-value for state–action pair (s,a), α is the learning rate, and R is the reward for taking action a in state s. The variable γ is the discount factor, a value between 0 and 1, which discounts future rewards in relation to immediate rewards.

The game we model in our simulation also assumes that players have beliefs regarding various aspects of the game. After each round, the players update their beliefs with Bayesian updating using a function that uses the Beta distribution to update the beliefs of each player based on their observed rewards. The beliefs of the players are represented by the parameters *alpha* and *beta* of the Beta distribution. The parameter *alpha* represents the number of successes (rewards) and the parameter *beta* represents the number of failures (punishments) for each player. As the players observe the rewards and punishments received during the game, their beliefs are updated, reflecting their understanding of the underlying environment and the unobserved confounder's influence. Although the players' beliefs are updated using Bayesian methods, the strategy selection and action–value updates are based on Q-learning and SARSA for Players 1 and 2, respectively. While players learn to adjust their strategies based on the rewards they receive, they do not explicitly take the unobserved confounder into account in their decision-making process. With the model setup in place, let us now take a look at some simulations.

Before we analyze a fully fleshed-out version of the game, we first examine a simpler variant of it where the state of the economy can be observed by the players. In Figure 5.5, we see the results of this game in a simulation over twenty rounds and ten thousand iterations.

The first thing we note in Figure 5.5 is that the average payoffs are almost identical, with SARSA showing itself to be marginally more advantageous overall. Thus, with an observable state and fixed payoffs, there is not much difference between the two algorithms. Now, let us observe the results when we hide the state of the economy and also allow the payoffs to vary. For example, instead of a standard

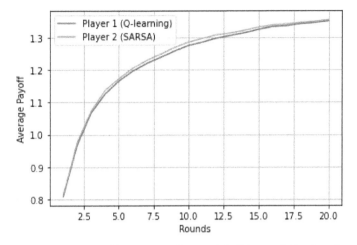

Figure 5.5. Trade Negotiation Game with Observed Confounder.

		Player 2	
		Policy 1	Policy 2
Player 1	Policy 1	[2,5], [1,4]	0, 0
	Policy 2	0, 0	[1,4], [2,5]

Figure 5.6. Modified Battles of the Sexes.

payoff matrix in the Battle of the Sexes game, we allow payoffs to fall in a range, as in Figure 5.6.

We similarly modify the Prisoner's Dilemma in our simulation to allow for ranges in the payoffs. The payoff matrix for this modified version of the Prisoner's Dilemma game is shown in Figure 5.7.

In Figure 5.8, we show the results of a simulation with the unobserved state (confounder) and varying payoffs. Our first observation is that the average payoffs for both algorithms are significantly lower than those shown in Figure 5.5. This is due to the unobserved nature of the confounder, which makes decision-making more difficult. Moreover, given that we have variance in the payoffs for various actions, learning the precise structure of each game is also more challenging.

		Player 2	
Player 1		Cooperate	Defect
	Cooperate	[2,4], [2,4]	0, [5,8]
	Defect	[5,8], 0	[1,3], [1,3]

Figure 5.7. Modified Prisoner's Dilemma.

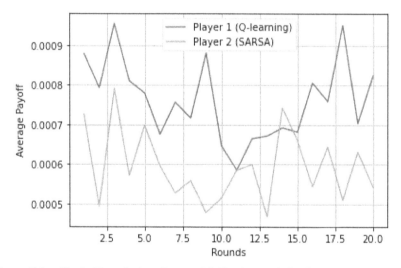

Figure 5.8. Trade Negotiation Game with Unobserved Confounder and Varying Payoffs.

Our other major observation is that Q-learning performs significantly better than SARSA in this version of the game. This is likely because Q-learning is less sensitive to the high variance in rewards compared to SARSA. In Q-learning, the updates to the Q-values are based on the maximum Q-value of the next state–action pair, which can be advantageous in situations with high payoff variance. The Q-values are thus more likely to converge to the optimal values in such an environment. In addition, the presence of an unobserved confounder can introduce hidden dependencies between actions, rewards, and states. Q-learning's exploration mechanism can help it adapt to these hidden dependencies and better capture the underlying dynamics of the environment, leading to improved performance.

5.4 The Noisy-OR Model

In artificial intelligence (AI), graph theoretical structures have become a popular way to represent causal relations. For example, a *Causal network* (CN) is a type of *Bayesian network* (BN) that is used to model the conditional dependencies of variables in a DAG and draw inferences based on their probabilistic relations.[14] In many real-life problems, we are confronted with situations where there is likely to be more than one possible cause for an observed effect. In such cases, researchers require a framework to efficiently model the interaction of several causes and their aggregate impact on the realization of effects.

While basic versions of BNs can model several causes simultaneously, the question of efficiency is of prime importance in more expansive models. This is because, in BNs, each node with a parent has a conditional probability table (CPT) associated with it that contains a set of discrete probability distributions corresponding to all possible combinations of parent states. For example, in a binary model (with two possible states for each parent) where a variable x has five parents, the CPT associated with x will have $2^5 = 32$ probability distributions. Thus, the number of parameters in a CPT increases exponentially as the number of parents increases. Thus, BNs can be computationally expensive when a model is of sufficient complexity.

In response to the foregoing challenge, the *noisy-OR* (NOR) model has been introduced.[15] NOR is a probabilistic variant of the disjunction connective ∨ from deductive logic. To simplify the computational operations in BNs, the NOR model gives a causal interpretation of the relationship between parent and child nodes and assumes that causes act independently of one another in terms of their ability to influence the actualization of effects. This allows the

---

[14] Bayesian networks are also known as *belief networks*.
[15] The noisy-OR model originated in the work of Good (1961), Peng and Reggia (1986), and Pearl (1988).

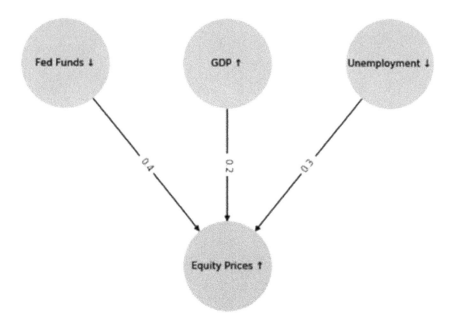

Figure 5.9. Noisy-OR Probability DAG.

compound effect of multiple causes to be modeled in a linear fashion. Both positive (promoting) and negative (inhibiting) causes can be evaluated using the NOR model, allowing for an assessment of the net conditional probability of an effect.[16]

In Figure 5.9,[17] we show a visual depiction of the causal structure assumed by the NOR model. In the exhibit, the values on the edges of the graph indicate the causal probabilities of each individual cause before it interacts with the other causes in the model.

The NOR model encodes and quantifies causal beliefs in graphical form and assumes that causal mechanisms work independently of one

---

[16]The basic NOR model assumes that all causal influences are contained in a given model. However, Henrion (1987) introduced the notion of a *leak probability*, which is a non-zero probability for the effect to materialize even if all of the causes considered are not actualized. Díez (1993) and Srinivas (1993) extended the model to non-Boolean variables. Lemmer and Gossnik (2004) proposed a recursive version of the model that includes synergies among the causes.

[17]This example is taken from Simonian (2021).

another. In (5.15), we show the basic formal machinery for calculating the conditional probability for several causes of a single type, either positive or negative. In (5.16), we show how the probabilities for each type of cause can be aggregated to produce an all-things-considered probability of an effect materializing given our respective probability assignments to our sets of positive and negative causes. Positive and negative causes are, respectively, denoted by plus and minus sign superscripts:

$$P(E|\boldsymbol{C}) = 1 - \prod_{C_i \in \boldsymbol{C}} (1 - p_i). \qquad (5.15)$$

$$P(E|\boldsymbol{C}^+, \boldsymbol{C}^-) = \frac{P(E|\boldsymbol{C}^+) + 1 - P(\neg E|\boldsymbol{C}^-)}{2}. \qquad (5.16)$$

As an example of how NOR works, consider the case where there are two sets of causes that we believe promote or inhibit an appreciation in the stock price of a publicly listed US oil company (the effect). The set of prospective promoting causes includes (1) a cut in the federal funds rate following the next FOMC meeting, (2) a positive GDP print for the most recent quarter, and (3) a positive recent jobs report. The set of inhibiting causes includes (1) a proposed profit tax on energy companies by some members of Congress, (2) the potential for OPEC to raise production quotas, and (3) a new set of proposed regulations by the Environmental Protection Agency (EPA) that may restrict drilling rights and operations. In Table 5.2, we show the NOR operations for each set of causes given specific probability assignments for each cause.

With the values from Table 5.2 in hand, we proceed to calculate the value of (5.16). If we assign True to the truth values of all positive and negative causes, then the value of (5.16) in this case is

$$P(E|\boldsymbol{C}^+, \boldsymbol{C}^-) = \frac{0.664 + 1 - 0.622}{2} = 0.521. \qquad (5.17)$$

One notable feature of the NOR model is that the mere presence of an additional cause in a disjunction is often enough to materially raise the probability of an effect materializing, even when low probability values have been assigned to each individual cause. In our example, low probability values were deliberately chosen for each of the causes

Table 5.2. Noisy-OR Probability Tables.

Panel A: Probabilities for Promoting Causes

Fed Funds ↓	GDP ↑	Unemployment ↓	P(Stock Price ↑)	$P_\neg$ (Stock Price ↑)
False	False	False	0	1
False	False	True	0.3	0.7
False	True	False	0.2	0.8
False	True	True	0.44	$0.56 = 0.7 \times 0.8$
True	False	False	0.4	0.6
True	False	True	0.58	$0.42 = 0.7 \times 0.6$
True	True	False	0.52	$0.48 = 0.8 \times 0.6$
'	True	True	0.664	$0.336 = 0.7 \times 0.8 \times 0.6$

Panel B: Probabilities for Inhibiting Causes

Profit Tax ↑	OPEC Quotas ↑	Regulations ↑	$P_\neg$ (Stock Price ↑)	P (Stock Price ↑)
False	False	False	0	1
False	False	True	0.1	0.9
False	True	False	0.4	0.6
False	True	True	0.58	$0.42 = 0.6 \times 0.7$
True	False	False	0.3	0.7
True	False	True	0.37	$0.63 = 0.9 \times 0.7$
True	True	False	0.46	$0.54 = 0.9 \times 0.6$
True	True	True	0.622	$0.378 = 0.9 \times 0.6 \times 0.7$

to illustrate this point. As Table 5.2 shows, in the bottom row of each panel, where each cause takes a truth value of True, the resulting probability value is above 0.50 even though in each case, all three constituent causes have a probability assignment below 0.50.

We note that while the sources of the probability assignments in the NOR model may vary, they are often derived from some type of expert opinion. For example, imagine a healthcare setting where a medical professional assigns probability values based on their belief in the cause-and-effect relationship between various diseases and a particular symptom that has been observed in a patient.

We also note that aside from the standard NOR model, there are several variants that can help add more sophistication to causal analysis. For example, in a *weighted NOR*,[18] some causes are assumed to have stronger or more influential effects. The weighted NOR model thus assigns different weights or strengths to each cause, allowing for variations in their contributions to the outcome. Another variation of the NOR is the *threshold NOR*,[19] which introduces a threshold parameter that determines the minimum number of active causes required to produce an outcome. It assumes that the outcome occurs only if a certain number or proportion of causes are active or present. This variant captures the idea that the outcome is influenced by a critical mass or combination of causes. The *hierarchical NOR*[20] considers a hierarchical structure of causes, where higher-level causes affect the activation of lower-level causes. It allows for the capturing of complex dependencies and interactions among causes at different levels, enabling a more detailed representation of causal relationships. Finally, the *temporal NOR*[21] incorporates temporal dynamics and time-dependent factors into the model. It accounts for the fact that cause-and-effect relationships may evolve and that causes may have different levels of influence on an outcome over time. Temporal NOR models should be of special interest to economists and investors as economic and market phenomena often have causal relationships marked by dynamic temporal dependencies.

We now provide a simulation where we show how NOR models can be combined with reinforcement learning and game theory to assist us in macro investing. In our example, two portfolio managers must decide how much capital to allocate to three countries in successive rounds in accordance with their assessment of how likely it is that each country will have a strong economy. What determines whether a country's economy will be strong or not is a NOR model, whose structure is observable to both players. The model we use assumes that the strength of a country's economy is a function of three contributing causes: price stability (inflation), political stability, and high labor productivity.

---

[18] For more on weighted belief networks see Henrion (1987).
[19] For a threshold belief model see Jurgelenaite *et al.* (2006).
[20] For more on hierarchies in belief networks see Henrion (1987).
[21] For more on the temporal aspects of belief networks see Dean and Kanazawa (1989) and Nicholson and Brady (1994).

Allocating resources in the manner described above can be modeled as what is known as a *Colonel Blotto game*.[22] This game is a two-player, zero-sum game where each player allocates a fixed budget of resources across multiple battlefields without knowledge of the opponent's choices. The player who allocates more resources to a specific battlefield wins it, and the overall winner is determined by a majority of victories across all battlefields. Our simulation extends the standard Blotto game by utilizing Multi-armed Bandit (MB) algorithms to drive each player's actions over time. Specifically, the NOR-derived probabilities are interpreted as arms in a MB model, discussed in previous chapters. As the simulation progresses, the bandit algorithms guide the players in choosing how much capital to allocate to each country in each round. We also introduce a hidden confounder, a variable that is unobservable to the players but alters the NOR-derived probability by scaling it up or down by the hidden variable value. We can consider this variable as representing an economic shock of some type. This hidden variable represents the uncertainty attached to the causal model associated with each country. Again, it is a confounder because it influences both the strategies that players choose and the payoffs accruing to each player, which are also influenced by the strategies that the players adopt. Given the foregoing characteristics, our simulation can be considered another example of causal reinforcement learning.

In our game, each portfolio manager is assumed to have the same amount of capital. At the beginning of the simulation, the managers utilize a set of initial probabilities to determine where to allocate their resources. These probabilities represent the beliefs or expectations of each player regarding the likelihood of a country's economy being strong. For example, suppose the players each have 100 units of capital to allocate among three countries. In the first round, Manager 1 allocates 60 units to Country 1, 20 units to Country 2, and 20 units to Country 3. Manager 2, on the other hand, allocates 40 units to Country 1, 40 units to Country 2, and 20 units to Country 3. Then, the strength of the economy for each country is calculated based on the NOR model and the winner is determined. For example, in round one, if Country 1 has a strong economy and Country 2 and Country 3 do not, then Manager 1 wins and Manager 2 loses.

---

[22] For background information on Blotto games, see Borel (1921), Rapoport and Guyer (1966), Brams (1994), and Epstein and Heizler (2001).

Causal Inference in Models of Strategic Interaction 117

Table 5.3. Thompson Sampling Algorithm.

Let K be the number of arms in a Multi-armed Bandit.
- The unknown true reward probability of arm k is denoted as θ_k where k ranges from 0 to 1.
- For each arm k, the prior distribution is represented as Beta(α_k, β_k).
- α_k and β_k are the hyperparameters of the Beta distribution, representing prior successes and failures, respectively.

The algorithm proceeds as follows:

(1) At each time step t, Thompson sampling samples a reward probability from the posterior distribution for each arm k based on the observed rewards up to time t. The arm with the highest sampled reward probability is selected for the current time step.

- Let $X_k(t)$ be the number of reward occurrences for arm k up to time t.
- Let $N_k(t)$ be the number of arm pulls for arm k up to time t.
  The posterior distribution for arm k at time t is given by the following:
  Posterior$(\theta_k | X_k(t), N_k(t)) \sim$ Beta$(\alpha_k + X_k(t), \beta_k + N_k(t) - X_k(t))$.

(2) Once the arm is selected based on the sampled posterior probabilities, the player pulls the selected arm.
(3) The player observes the reward (success or failure) and updates the number of successes and trials for that arm.
(4) The algorithm continues for multiple time steps, with arm selection, pulling, and updates at each step.

We present two simulations to examine our game. In each simulation, we assume that the managers use different algorithms to guide their decision-making. Manager 1 uses the UCB algorithm described in Chapter 2, while Manager 2 uses an algorithm known as *Thompson Sampling*. We describe the formal machinery of Thompson sampling in Table 5.3.

We now present our two simulations. In the first, we assume that there is a low level of uncertainty associated with our hidden confounder for each country. In other words, the hidden variable values fall into a narrow range. In our second case study, we assume a wider range for our hidden variable. Our goal is to understand which learning algorithm performs better in each study and to draw conclusions on their practical applicability.

Moving on to our first simulation, we first present our input values. Our probability assignments are as follows:

- The initial player probability assignments regarding the likelihood of a country's economic strength are as follows:
  - Player 1 = [Country 1: 0.4, Country 2: 0.5, Country 3: 0.1],
  - Player 2 = [Country 1: 0.3, Country 2: 0.4, Country 3: 0.3].
- Probability of a strong economy | price stability : [Country 1: 0.8, Country 2: 0.7, Country 3: 0.6].
- Probability of a strong economy | political stability : [Country 1: 0.6, Country 2: 0.9, Country 3: 0.5].
- Probability of a strong economy | high labor productivity : [Country 1: 0.7, Country 2: 0.5, Country 3: 0.8].
- For our hidden variable ranges, we have the following: [Country 1: (0.5, 0.6), Country 2: (0.2, 0.3), Country 3: (0.6, 0.8)].

We assume that each player allocates one hundred units of capital in each of ten rounds. We iterate the simulation one thousand times, then calculate and plot the average number of wins for each player for each round of the game. As we see in Figure 5.10, in a situation with low model uncertainty, the UCB algorithm performs significantly better than Thompson sampling.

In our second simulation, we retain the input variable values from the first study, except the values for the hidden variables, which are modified as follows:

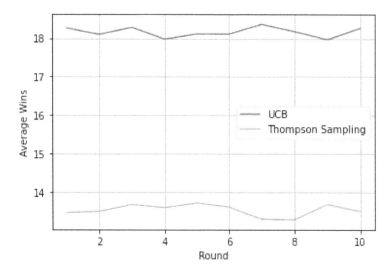

Figure 5.10.   NOR Bandit Study: Low Model Uncertainty.

Causal Inference in Models of Strategic Interaction 119

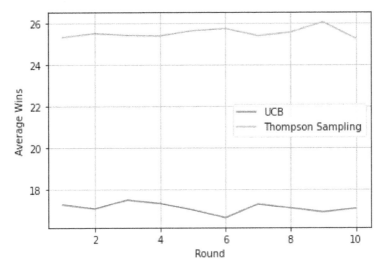

Figure 5.11. NOR Bandit Study: High Model Uncertainty.

Hidden variable ranges (second case study) = [Country 1: (0.5, 1.1), Country 2: (0.2, 0.8), Country 3: (0.7, 1.3)].

As we see in Figure 5.11., Thompson sampling seems to be better suited for situations where the reward distributions of the arms are not well known or are uncertain. This could be because it models the uncertainty using Bayesian probability, which allows players to better update and adapt their strategies based on the rewards and punishments they receive from their actions. It could also be because Thompson sampling tends to strike a better balance between exploration and exploitation. This is particularly advantageous in situations where the underlying reward distributions of the arms are highly uncertain or changing over time.

5.5 Strategic Decision-making Under Causal Ignorance

Understanding the causal relations that drive macro developments is integral to making sound investment decisions. However, given the challenges in understanding causal relations in political and economic systems, we are faced with a situation in which, despite our best efforts, we may not be able to precisely discern the causal structure of the events that are relevant to our decision-making process.

Given the foregoing epistemic challenges, it would seem that when making economically relevant decisions, agents should undertake courses of action that will likely produce economic gains under a number of causal scenarios. Whether the goal is to craft economic policy or manage a portfolio, decisions that are likely to "work" in a number of different causal scenarios have more utility than those that are tailored to specific sequences of events. However, in order to make decisions with the requisite level of general applicability, it is necessary to determine the similarities and differences among the causal scenarios considered. That is the aim of the framework described in the final section of this chapter.

5.5.1 A Causal Case Study

Consider a scenario in which the members of a portfolio management team are deliberating the effect of a recent fall in interest rates.[23] In order to craft an effective investment strategy, it is critical that the portfolio managers' decisions be driven by consideration of the most plausible economic and market scenarios. Let us assume that they are considering three possible causal schemes:

(1) Lower interest rates A cause an increase in consumer prices B and a rise in the stock market C. The real estate market D is unaffected.
(2) Lower interest rates A cause an increase in real estate prices D, but do not cause an increase in consumer prices B or a rise in the stock market C.
(3) Lower interest rates A cause a rise in the stock market C and an increase in real estate prices D, but do not cause a rise in consumer prices B.

---

[23]Some of the material in this section is adapted from that originally presented in Simonian (2022).

These scenarios are represented graphically in the following manner:

$$G_1: A \to B, A \to C, D.$$
$$G_2: A \to D, B, C.$$
$$G_3: A \to C, A \to D, B.$$

Whichever one of the above-mentioned scenarios is accepted as the correct causal description of the observed events will form the basis of the ultimate course of action adopted by the portfolio managers. Now, if we assume that it is impossible to craft a single investment strategy or trade that will benefit equally in all three scenarios, then it would be prudent to invest according to the scenario that has the highest "causal proximity" to the other scenarios. In this way, our investment strategy will presumably still be at least partially effective in case one of the other scenarios materializes.

To make sense of the idea of causal proximity, however, we first have to understand the notion of *causal dependence*. In general, the dependence between cause and effect can be construed as either *probabilistic dependence* or *counterfactual dependence*. These two concepts of causation form the basis of a procedure described by Eva *et al.* (2019) that allows us to determine the distance between causal graphs — DAGs over a set of events **V**.

We first consider probabilistic dependence,[24] which is based on the Causal Markov Condition (CMC), which states that, conditional on the set of all its direct causes, a node is independent of all variables that are not direct causes or direct effects of that node. The CMC thus provides a methodology for inferring probabilistic independencies from DAGs. The *probability distance* $dP(G, G^*)$ between two causal structures G and G^* is measured by counting the number of conditional independencies that are entailed by one but not both of G and G^*, normalized by the total number of possible conditional independencies that could hold between the variable set **V**.

---

[24]Eva *et al.* (2019) call it "evidential similarity."

To determine Markov equivalence, we utilize the concept of directed separation (d-separation), which tells us whether two nodes are independent given a set of observed nodes. The concept of d-separation relies on three types of so-called *blocking* conditions. In a directed graph, such as a DAG, a path is considered blocked if there is a set of observed variables that impede the flow of information along the path, making the two variables conditionally independent. On the other hand, a path is considered unblocked if there is no such blocking set of observed variables, indicating a dependence between the variables. The first blocking condition is for a *collider*, a node on the path where both incoming edges meet. In this case, the path is blocked unless the collider itself or one of its descendants is observed. The second blocking condition is for a *non-collider*, a node where only one incoming edge exists. In this case, the path is blocked if the non-collider is observed. Finally, we have a *chain*, a consecutive sequence of non-colliders on the path. In this case, the path is open unless one of the nodes in the chain is observed, in which case the path becomes blocked.

To determine the Markov equivalence between two DAGs, you would need to check if they have the same set of d-separations or conditional independence relations. It is a graphical criterion that determines whether or not two variables are conditionally independent, given a third set of observed variables, in a directed graphical model. To help us determine the Markov equivalence and probabilistic distance between two DAGs, we use what is known as the *Orientation Discovery Algorithm*, which we outline in Table 5.4.

We next consider counterfactual dependence. Counterfactual dependence is focused on the idea that causes are difference makers, in the sense that *if cause C were (or had been) the case, effect E would be (or have been) the case.*[25] For two causal structures G and G^* over a variable set $\mathbf{V}$, the *counterfactual distance* $dC(G, G^*)$ between them is determined by counting all those possible counterfactual dependencies about which G and G^* disagree and normalizing by the cardinality of the set of possible counterfactual dependencies among $\mathbf{V}$. We show this procedure in Table 5.5.

---

[25]The classic account of counterfactual causation is provided by Lewis (1973).

Table 5.4. Orientation Discovery Algorithm.

(1) Initialization: For a given graph G with nodes $V = \{X_1, X_2, \ldots, X_i\}$, for each node X_i, initialize the parents of a node $pa(X)$ and children of $ch(X_i)$ as empty sets.
(2) Update the sets $pa(X_i)$ and $ch(X_i)$ for each node X_i as follows:
$pa(X_i) = \{X_j | X_i \text{ is } d\text{-separated from } X_j \text{ given } pa(X_j)\}$.
$ch(X_i) = \{X_j | X_j \text{ is } d\text{-separated from } X_i \text{ given } ch(X_i)\}$.
(3) The normalized orientation distance is calculated as follows:
Let $pa(G, X_i)$ denote the set of parent nodes of X_i in graph G.
Let $ch(G, X_i)$ denote the set of child nodes of X_i in graph G.
(4) The orientation distance (OD) between graphs G_1 and G_2 is given by the following:

$$OD(G_1, G_2) = \sum_{X_i \in V} (\delta(pa(G_1, X_i), pa(G_2, X_i)) + \delta(ch(G_1, X_i), ch(G_2, X_i))),$$

where $\delta(A, B)$ is the Kronecker delta function, which is defined as

$$\delta(A, B) = \begin{cases} 1, & \text{if } A \neq B \\ 0, & \text{if } A = B \end{cases}.$$

The orientation distance OD thus computes the sum of differences between the sets of parent and child nodes for each node in the graphs. If the sets of parents or children for a particular node differ between the graphs, the Kronecker delta function assigns a value of 1 to that contribution, indicating a difference. Otherwise, if the sets are the same, the function assigns a value of 0, indicating no difference.
(5) The normalized orientation distance NOD between graphs G_1 and G_2 is given by the following:

$$NOD(G_1, G_2) = \frac{OD(G_1, G_2)}{|N|},$$

where $OD(G_1, G_2)$ is the orientation distance between graphs G_1 and G_2 and $|N|$ is the cardinality of the set N, representing the total number of nodes in the graphs. The value of the NOD falls between 0 and 1. A NOD value of 0 implies that the two graphs are Markov equivalent.

Table 5.5. Counterfactual Distance Algorithm.

(1) Given a set of nodes V, we define two lists, $list_1 = [x_1, x_2, \ldots, x_n]$ and $list_2 = [y_1, y_2, \ldots, y_n]$, with each list containing a finite set of counterfactual dependencies, e.g., A < B. We also define a reference list $ref = [z_1, z_2, \ldots, z_n]$ containing all possible counterfactual dependencies.
(2) For each counterfactual dependency z_i in ref present in both $list_1$ and $list_2$, or absent in both $list_1$ and $list_2$, add z_i to a new list, *shared elements*.
(3) For each counterfactual dependency z_i in ref present in $list_1$ or $list_2$, but not the other, add z_i to a new list, *unshared elements*.
(4) Compute the normalized counterfactual distance (NCD) as the ratio of unshared items, labeled the *unshared elements count*, to the total number of possible counterfactual dependencies, labeled the ref count:

$$\text{NCD} = \frac{\text{unshared elements count}}{\text{ref count}}.$$

To summarize, the algorithm iterates through the reference list, checking for the presence of tuples in both lists and calculating the counts of shared and unshared items. It then computes the normalized distance as the ratio of unshared items to the total number of items in the reference list.

Table 5.6. Summary of Probabilistic and Counterfactual Distances Between Causal Graphs.

	$d_P(-,-)$	$d_C(-,-)$
G_1, G_2	1/4	1/4
G_1, G_3	0	1/6
G_2, G_3	1/4	1/12

Now, we are able calculate both probabilistic and counterfactual distances for graphs G_1, G_2, and G_3, which we show in Table 5.6.

How do we choose between the probabilistic and counterfactual frameworks based on the results in Table 5.6? Eva *et al.* (2019) suggested two approaches: (1) In the *lexicographic* approach, first either the probabilistic or counterfactual distance is used to narrow down the set of alternative causal schemes and then the distance measure not used initially is used as a tiebreaker among the remaining schemes. (2) In the *weighted approach*, the probabilistic and counterfactual distance values for each candidate scheme are weighted, and the scheme that has the lowest sum distance is used. Because we are assuming that agents make decisions from the standpoint of maximal causal ignorance, we advocate taking the total sum distance of each causal scheme as its *total distance score*. This is essentially the same as using the weighted decision scheme with a 0.50 weight attached to each distance measure and so does not assume any special information regarding the relative correctness of either of the distance measures. Using this methodology, we see in Table 5.6 that G_3 has the lowest total distance score of 0.50, followed by G_1 with a score of 0.66 and G_2 with a score of 0.83. Thus, if we are forced to choose one causal scheme to guide our investment decisions, it would be G_3.

5.6 Concluding Points

Causal relations, as opposed to mere correlations, are an important aspect of decision-making in any domain, including investing. This chapter has provided a detailed overview of various aspects of causal inference that are relevant to the analysis of geopolitical questions. Like in previous chapters, we have also demonstrated how causal considerations can be incorporated into simulations of strategic interaction. Now that we have examined a full range of game types and computational techniques that can be applied to geopolitical analysis, it is important to consider how geopolitical views can be expressed in investment portfolios. Accordingly, in Chapter 6, we will provide a detailed account of various portfolio construction frameworks and demonstrate how to utilize the results of geopolitical analysis as inputs into the portfolio selection process.

References

Angrist, J.D. and Krueger, A.B. 1999. Empirical strategies in labor economics. In *Handbook of Labor Economics*, Ashenfelter, O. and Card D. (eds.), Vol. 3A. Amsterdam: North-Holland.

Angrist, J.D. and Krueger, A.B. 2001. Instrumental variables and the search for identification: From supply and demand to natural experiments. *Journal of Economic Perspectives* 15(4): 69–85.

Bareinboim, E., Forney, A. and Pearl, J. 2015. Bandits with unobserved confounders: A Causal Approach. In *Proceedings of the 28th Annual Conference on Neural Information Processing Systems*.

Borel, E. 1921. La Théorie Du Jeu et Les Équations Intégrales à Noyau Symétrique. *Comptes Rendus de l'Académie des Sciences* 173: 1304–1308. English translation by Leonard J. Savage, 1953, *Econometrica* 21(1): 97–100.

Brams, S.J. 1994. The colonel blotto game. *Mathematics Magazine* 67(5): 295–307.

Collingwood, R.G. 1940. *An Essay on Metaphysics.* Oxford: Clarendon Press, Oxford.

Cook, T.D. and Campbell, D.T. 1979. *Quasi-Experimentation: Design and Analysis Issues for Field Settings.* Boston: Houghton Mifflin Company.

Dean, T., and Kanazawa, K. 1989. A model for reasoning about persistence and causation. *Computational Intelligence*, 5(3), 142–150.

Díez, F.J. 1993. Parameter adjustment in Bayes networks. The generalized noisy OR-gate. In *UAI '93: Proceedings of the Ninth Annual Conference on Uncertainty in Artificial Intelligence*, 99–105. San Francisco: Morgan Kaufmann.

Epstein, G.S. and Heizler, O. 2001. Colonel blotto in the field: A laboratory study of two-player games. *RAND Journal of Economics* 32(3): 502–516.

Eva, B., Stern, R. and Hartmann, S. 2019. The similarity of causal structure. *Philosophy of Science* 86 (5): 821–835.

Favero, C. and Hendry, D.F. 1992. Testing the lucas critique: A review. *Econometric Reviews* 11(3): 265–306.

Gasking, D. 1955. Causation and Recipes. *Mind* 64(256): 479–487.

Good, I.J. 1961. A Causal Calculus (I). *British Journal of Philosophy of Science* 11(44): 305–318.

Granger, C.W.J. 1969. Investigating causal relations by econometric models and cross-spectral methods. *Econometrica* 37(3): 424–438.

Hausman, D.M. 1986. Causation and experimentation. *American Philosophical Quarterly* 23(2): 143–154.

Hausman, D.M. 1998. *Causal Asymmetries.* Cambridge: Cambridge University Press.

Henrion, M. 1987. Some practical issues in constructing belief networks. In *Proceedings of the Annual Conference on Uncertainty in Artificial Intelligence (UAI-87).* Elsevier Science.

Hicks, J. 1979. *Causality in Economics.* Oxford: Basil Blackwell, Oxford.

Hood, W. and Koopmans, T. 1953. Studies in econometric method (eds.). *Cowles Commission Monograph No. 14.* New Haven: Yale University Press.

Hoover, K.D. 1990. The logic of causal inference: Econometrics and the conditional analysis of causality. *Economics and Philosophy* 6(2): 207–234.

Hoover, K.D. 2001. *Causality in Macroeconomics.* Cambridge: Cambridge University Press.
Hoover, K.D. 2008. Causality in economics and econometrics. In *The New Palgrave Dictionary of Economics,* Durlauf, S.N. and Blume, L.E. (eds.), Vol. 1. London: Palgrave Macmillan.
Hume, D. 1902. *Enquiries Concerning the Human Understanding and Concerning the Principles of Morals,* 2nd edition. Selby-Bigge, L.A. (eds.), Oxford: Clarendon Press, Oxford 1777.
Jurgelenaite, R., Lucas, P., and Heskes, T. 2006. Exploring the noisy threshold function in designing bayesian networks. In: Bramer, M., Coenen, F., Allen, T. (eds) *Research and Development in Intelligent Systems XXII. SGAI 2005.* Springer, London.
Koopmans, T. 1950. *Statistical Inference in Dynamic Economic Models,* Cowles Commission Monograph No. 10. New York: Wiley.
Lee, S. and Bareinboim, E. 2019. Structural causal bandits with non-manipulable variables. In *Proceedings of the 33rd AAAI Conference on Artificial Intelligence.*
Lemmer, J.F. and Gossink, D.E. 2004. Recursive Noisy Or — A rule for estimating complex probabilistic interactions. *IEEE Transactions on Systems, Man, and Cybernetics,* Part B 34(6): 2252–2261.
Menzies, P. and Price, H. 1993. Causation as a secondary quality. *British Journal for the Philosophy of Science* 44(2): 187–203.
Nicholson, A. E. and Brady, J. M. 1994. Dynamic belief networks for discrete monitoring, in *IEEE Transactions on Systems, Man, and Cybernetics* 24(11): 1593–1610.
Pearl, J. 1988. *Probabilistic Reasoning in Intelligent Systems: Networks of Plausible Inference.* San Francisco: Morgan Kaufmann.
Pearl J. 2009. *Causality: Models, Reasoning, and Inference.* 2nd edition. New York: Cambridge University Press.
Peng, Y. and Reggia, J.A. 1986. Plausibility of diagnostic hypotheses: The nature of simplicity. In *Proceedings of the 5th National Conference on AI (AAAI-86),* pp. 140–145.
Rapoport, A. and Guyer, M.J. 1966. A taxonomy of 2 × 2 games. *General Systems* 11: 203–214.
Rummery, G.A. and Niranjan, M. 1994. *On-line Q-Learning using Connectionist Systems* [Technical Report]. Cambridge University Engineering Department.
Simon, H.A. 1953. Causal order and identifiability. In *Studies in Econometric Methods,* Hood, W.C. and Koopmans, T.C. New York: John Wiley & Sons.

Simonian, J., de Prado, M. and Fabozzi, F. 2018. INVITED EDITORIAL COMMENT: Order from chaos: How data Science is revolutionizing investment practice. *The Journal of Portfolio Management* 45(1): 1–4.

Simonian, J. and Fabozzi, F. 2019. Triumph of the empiricists: The birth of financial data science. *The Journal of Financial Data Science* 1(1): 10–13.

Simonian, J. 2021. Causal uncertainty in capital markets: A robust Noisy-Or framework for portfolio management. *Journal of Financial Data Science* 3(1): 43–55.

Simonian, J. 2022. Investment decisions under almost complete causal ignorance. *The Journal of Portfolio Management* 49(1): 33–38.

Sims, C.A. 1980. Macroeconomics and Reality. *Econometrica* 48(1): 1–48.

Spirtes, P. and Glymour, C. 1991. An algorithm for fast recovery of sparse causal graphs. *Social Science Computer Review* 9(1): 62–72.

Srinivas, S. 1993. A generalization of the Noisy-OR model. In *UAI '93: Proceedings of the Ninth Annual Conference on Uncertainty in Artificial Intelligence*, 208–218.

Sutton, R.S. and Barto, A.G. 2018. *Reinforcement Learning: An Introduction.* Cambridge, MA: MIT Press.

von Wright, G.H. 1971. *Explanation and Understanding.* Ithaca, NY: Cornell University Press.

Woodward, J. 2003. *Making Things Happen.* Oxford: Oxford University Press.

Zellner, A.A. 1979. Causality and econometrics. In *Three Aspects of Policy Making: Knowledge, Data and Institutions*, Brunner, K. and Meltzer, A.H. (eds.), Carnegie-Rochester Conference Series on Public Policy, Vol. 10. Amsterdam: North-Holland.

Chapter 6

Portfolio Construction

6.1 The Final Piece of the Puzzle

In the previous chapters, we have shown how game theory, reinforcement learning, and causal inference can be used to inform geopolitical analysis and in doing so help foster the development of more precise macro views. However, determining one's investment views is but one aspect of the portfolio management process. Indeed, to fully demonstrate the practical utility of the ideas presented, we need to show how geopolitical and macro views, once formed, can be expressed during portfolio construction. By *portfolio construction*, we mean the determination of asset weights in a portfolio. This is the focus of the present chapter.

So, how do we incorporate geopolitical views in actual portfolios? While it is possible to determine portfolio weights in an ad hoc or informal manner without utilizing formal portfolio optimization techniques, doing so might introduce several limitations and drawbacks. In the first place, ad hoc decision-making can lead to inconsistent portfolio adjustments, as decisions might be influenced by short-term market movements and information. This can result in frequent changes to the portfolio, increasing transaction costs and potentially undermining a portfolio manager's long-term strategy. Ad hoc decisions are also susceptible to biases and individual emotions. Investors might become overly attached to particular assets or make impulsive decisions based on market noise.

Mathematically driven portfolio optimization, on the other hand, is less prone to such manager biases and emotions. Another advantage of constructing portfolios using optimization is its potential utility in managing the various risks in a portfolio. Without precise calibration and management of market exposures, a portfolio could become overly exposed to certain risks, leading to larger losses during adverse market conditions. Further, portfolio optimization can also help investors maximize returns for a given level of risk or minimize risk for a desired level of return, ensuring a more efficient risk–return trade-off.

Aside from investment-related advantages, optimization offers investors implementation-related benefits. Ad hoc investment decision-making often consumes more time and effort as investors typically need to continually reassess and adjust their portfolios due to short-term market movements. Portfolio optimization, on the other hand, can help streamline the investment decision-making process and optimize resource allocation. Optimization methods can also assist investors in managing more complex portfolios. Informal approaches to portfolio allocation can prove to be challenging as more assets, factors, risks, and constraints are considered.

Finally, when the asset weights in a portfolio are determined via optimization, articulating the portfolio construction process to stakeholders and colleagues will generally be easier relative to explaining asset weights that were derived informally. This is due to the transparency and clear methodological basis that is typical of quantitative portfolio construction frameworks.

This chapter will review various portfolio optimization frameworks, both well-known frameworks and more novel approaches. We round out our discussion by providing an overview of two important topics. First, we present a game theoretic approach to aggregating multiple investor views. Given that most investment decisions are in practice informed by more than one individual, understanding how multiple views can be aggregated in a rigorous and nuanced manner is important. Second, we describe a machine learning driven approach to creating synthetic data with which to test portfolio robustness under different market scenarios. Ensuring portfolio robustness is the foundation of investment model validation and is critical for reliable portfolio construction given the pervasive risk of overfitting and model misspecification when applying quantitative methods.

6.2 Linear Programming

There is of course no shortage of portfolio construction methodologies. We start this chapter by showing how a familiar optimization framework, linear programming,[1] can be used to incorporate geopolitical views into the portfolio construction process. We then proceed to discuss how more sophisticated methods can be used to express geopolitical views during portfolio construction.

To begin, let us assume that we have a portfolio of five assets, two of which are vehicles that track the market indices in two distinct countries, ETFs, for example. The precise nature of each of the other three assets is not important. Let us further assume that we have developed a bearish view of the two country-specific assets based on geopolitical considerations. In the simplest case, we would exclude them from our portfolio altogether. However, even in this case, we would still be left with the challenge of reducing the correlation of our portfolio with the excluded country indices while simultaneously pursuing other portfolio goals related to risk and return.

In (6.1), we show a way to approach the foregoing challenge within a basic linear programming framework. As we see in the formulation of the problem, the optimization is a constrained maximization problem, with maximizing portfolio return as the objective function. With regard to constraints, the first two listed constraints require that the weighted sum of the Pearson correlations of the assets in the portfolio to each of the two excluded assets be less than 0.2 and 0.3, respectively. The third listed constraint requires that the weighted sum of the asset betas (linear sensitivities) to a stated benchmark be less than 0.8. The fourth constraint is that the portfolio weights sum to 1. The final two constraints set the lower and upper bounds

---

[1] For foundational papers on linear programming, see Khachiyan (1979) and Karmarkar (1984).

of the portfolio assets, respectively.

$$\begin{aligned}
\text{Maximize} \quad & 0.04x_1 + 0.03x_2 + 0.07x_3, \\
\text{s.t.} \quad & 0.2x_1 + 0.1x_2 + 0.4x_3 \leq 0.2, \\
& 0.1x_1 + 0.3x_2 + 0.3x_3 \leq 0.3, \\
& 0.60x_1 + 1.0x_2 + 0.85x_3 \leq 0.8, \\
& x_1 + x_2 + x_3 = 1, \\
& x_1, x_2, x_3 \geq 0.05, \\
& x_1, x_2, x_3 \leq 0.50.
\end{aligned} \qquad (6.1)$$

Running the optimization produces asset weights $\{x_1: 43\%, x_2: 38\%, x_3: 19\%\}$, with an expected return of 4.19%. We make two final points relating to the foregoing framework. First, it was not necessary to exclude the two unfavorably viewed country indices from the optimization. It is possible to include negatively viewed assets within the same optimization. The assets that a manager is bearish on may nevertheless be given zero weight by constraining them accordingly. Second, we can readily observe that including favorably viewed countries in the optimization only requires that the upper bound constraints relating to country-specific correlations be changed to lower bound constraints.

6.2.1 *Expressing Causal Views in Portfolios*

The foregoing optimization framework can also be used to build portfolios using more complex views involving causal relations. Recall the causal distance measures used to evaluate the similarity between causal schemes from the previous chapter. Once the sum causal distance of each causal scheme has been identified, we have in hand metrics which indicate the epistemic utility of each scheme. These metrics can in turn be used as inputs into optimizations to allocate among assets believed to benefit in case each causal scheme materializes. For example, let us assume that we have decided to make an active trade decision based on a consideration of the three causal graphs discussed in the previous chapter:

G_1: Lower interest rates A cause an increase in consumer prices B and a rise in the stock market C. The real estate market D is unaffected.

G_2: Lower interest rates A cause an increase in real estate prices D, but do not cause an increase in consumer prices B or a rise in the stock market C.

G_3: Lower interest rates A cause a rise in the stock market C and an increase in real estate prices D, but do not cause a rise in consumer prices B.

Let us assume that scheme G_1 supports an allocation to consumer staple stocks and an allocation away from private REITS, that scheme G_2 supports an allocation to private REITS and an allocation away from consumer staple stocks, and that scheme G_3 supports an allocation to public REITs and away from consumer staple stocks.

In the optimization shown in (6.2), we demonstrate one way of approaching the foregoing challenge within a linear programming framework. The example assumes that we would like to buy three securities and sell three securities for our portfolio based on our causal analysis. As we see in the formulation of the problem, the optimization is a constrained minimization problem, where minimizing the portfolio's total causal distance is the objective function. The total causal distance for each scheme is calculated using the values derived from Table 5.6 in Chapter 5 (G_1: 0.66, G_2: 0.83, G_3: 0.50). In terms of constraints, the first constraint requires that the sum of the trades equals 0 basis points. That is, the buys and the sells cancel each other out. The second and third constraints set upper and lower bounds on the total trade size, respectively. The fourth and fifth constraints set upper and lower bounds on the buys, while the sixth and seventh constraints set upper and lower bounds on the sells, respectively. Additional constraints could of course be added (e.g., relating to transaction costs), but we have kept the presentation simple for the sake of expository clarity.

$$\begin{aligned}
\text{Minimize} \quad & 0.66x_1 + 0.83x_2 + 0.50x_3 - 0.66x_4 - 0.83x_5 - 0.50x_6. \\
\text{s.t.} \quad & x_1 + x_2 + x_3 + x_4 + x_5 + x_6 = 0.0, \\
& x_1 + x_2 + x_3 \geq 0.04, \\
& x_1 + x_2 + x_3 \leq 0.05, \\
& x_1, x_2, x_3, \geq 0.005, \\
& x_1, x_2, x_3 \leq 0.05, \\
& x_4, x_5, x_6 \geq -0.02, \\
& x_4, x_5, x_6 \leq -0.005.
\end{aligned} \qquad (6.2)$$

Running the optimization produces the following set of trade sizes: $\{x_1: 0.5\%, x_2: 0.5\%, x_3: 3.0\%, x_4: -1.5\%, x_5: -0.5\%, x_6: -2.0\%\}$. Each of these weights corresponds to the pair trades indicated earlier. Specifically, the trades implied by this optimization are that 0.5% of our active trade budget should be used to buy consumer staple stocks and sell 1.5% of private REITs, buy 0.5% of private REITs and sell 0.5% of consumer staple stocks, and buy 3.0% of public REIT stocks and sell 2.0% of consumer staple stocks. Adding all the trades together, our final trades are to buy 3.0% of public REITs, sell 1.0% of private REITs, and sell 2.0% of consumer staple stocks. Of course, this is but one way in which buys and sells can be assigned. It is possible, for example, to assign unique pairs of trades to each graph or vary the number of buys and sells.

6.3 Quadratic Programming

6.3.1 *Mean–Variance Optimization*

Along with linear programming, the most popular framework for portfolio construction is quadratic programming. This is so because the most widespread portfolio construction framework, mean–variance optimization (MVO) (Markowitz, 1952), is solved using quadratic programming. The objective function of the mean–variance investor is expressed by the following:

$$\max_{w} w'\mu - \frac{\gamma}{2} w' \Sigma w,$$

with the optimal weights w satisfying

$$w = \frac{1}{\gamma} \sum\nolimits^{-1} \mu,$$

where μ represent asset returns, $\sum$ is the covariance matrix of assets, w represents the portfolio weights of each asset, and γ is the risk aversion parameter. We further note that, as is the case with linear programming, directional and/or causal views can be incorporated into both standard MVO and its extensions, such as the Black-Litterman model which we discuss next.

6.3.2 The Black–Litterman Model

Another popular portfolio allocation framework is the one proposed by Black and Litterman (1990, 1991, 1992). The Black–Litterman (BL) model provides a simple and transparent Bayesian framework for portfolio allocation, building on the foundation of the MVO.[2] The defining feature of the BL model is that it gives portfolio managers the ability to incorporate their forward-looking market views into the portfolio allocation process. For that reason, it presents an advantage over the MVO framework, as it provides the means to free portfolio managers from total reliance on historical data. For example, if a manager is attempting to build a global allocation, the BL model allows the portfolio manager to express views on specific countries in the portfolio. The views incorporated in the BL model might be driven by fundamental research or other quantitative models employed in the investment process.

In the traditional BL model, the portfolio manager reverse engineers the mean excess returns μ_0 by plugging in the relative weights of the assets in the benchmark portfolio w_0, as well as the values of a risk aversion parameter γ and the covariance matrix Σ:

$$\mu_0 = \gamma \sum w_0. \qquad (6.3)$$

The variance of the prior[3] on the mean[4] is then assumed to be proportional to the covariance matrix using a hyperparameter[5] τ, which in the context of active management applications of the BL model

---

[2]For a comprehensive overview of the BL model, see Kolm, et al. (2021).

[3]In Bayesian terminology, a *prior* is the probability distribution that represents an agent's beliefs about an uncertain parameter before consideration of any evidence.

[4]The underlying assumption of the model is that the returns are normally distributed (see Lee, 2000).

[5]The hyperparameter τ captures the difference between the variance–covariance matrix of historical and expected returns. A lower value for τ means that the variance of historical returns is higher than the variance of the expected returns

can be considered a measure of the portfolio manager's confidence in the benchmark portfolio or an expression of the manager's desired degree of active management. The reverse engineering process results in a prior that takes the form of a normal distribution with mean μ_0 and variance $\tau \sum$. An absence of views on the part of the portfolio manager results in the replication of the benchmark portfolio. As a portfolio manager introduces views on asset returns, the portfolio risk characteristics deviate from the benchmark in a manner consistent with mean–variance optimality.

The views of the portfolio manager employing the BL model are specified by building the matrices C and M such that the expected returns on each asset, here given by the vector μ_1, can be represented as follows:

$$C'\mu_1 = M. \qquad (6.4)$$

Additionally, the portfolio manager must specify the variance of his or her views. He and Litterman (1999) assumed that the variance of views is proportional to the variance of the asset returns, as in the case of the variance of the prior, thus setting $\Omega = \tau * \operatorname{diag}(C' \sum C)$. The resulting mean and covariance of the posterior distribution of asset returns is then expressed as follows:

$$\tilde{\mu} = \mu_0 + \tau \sum C [\tau(C' \sum C) + \Omega]^{-1} [M - C'\mu_0]. \qquad (6.5)$$

6.3.3 Ordinal Black–Litterman

In many portfolio management teams, precise return and risk forecasts are not used. Rather, assets are ranked or ordered in terms of their relative attractiveness with respect to various characteristics. Given this, it would be useful to adapt the BL model to accommodate an ordinal approach to portfolio selection. In this section, we demonstrate how this can be done. Ordinal Black–Litterman (OBL) is framed using variables that are similar to those used in the original BL framework, but in modified form. We describe these in Table 6.1.

---

and vice versa. In other words, the higher the confidence in benchmark returns, the lower the value of the hyperparameter. Because the variance of historical returns is usually higher than the variance of expected returns, the parameter τ will typically be assigned small values.

Table 6.1. Ordinal Black–Litterman Variables.

n is the number of assets in the portfolio.
w represents the vector of prior benchmark weights.
h represents the vector of historical security returns.
τ is the uncertainty parameter from the original BL model.
$\mathbf{P}_{returns}$ is the view matrix for ordinal views on returns. This is an identity matrix.
$\mathbf{Q}_{returns}$ is the vector of ordinal views on returns. Higher values indicate a preference for higher expected return assets.
$\mathbf{P}_{variances}$ is the view matrix for ordinal views on variances. This is an identity matrix.
$\mathbf{Q}_{variances}$ is the vector of ordinal views on variances. Higher values indicate a preference for lower variance assets.
$\mathbf{P}_{covariances}$ is the view matrix for ordinal views on covariances.
$\mathbf{Q}_{covariances}$ is the vector of ordinal views on covariances.
Higher values indicate a preference for more diversifying assets.
$\mathbf{C}_{prior}$ represents the prior covariance matrix.
$\mathbf{E}_{prior}$ represents the prior expected returns.
$\mathbf{I}$ is an identity matrix.

Now, we are in a position to show how to derive posterior values for our variances, expected returns, and covariance matrix:

$$\mathbf{V}_{posterior} = \mathbf{C}_{prior} + \tau(\mathbf{C}_{prior} - \tau \mathbf{C}_{prior} \mathbf{P}^T_{variances}(\mathbf{P}_{variances}\mathbf{C}_{prior}$$
$$\mathbf{P}^T_{variances} + \frac{1}{\tau}\mathbf{I})^{-1}\mathbf{P}_{variances}\mathbf{C}_{prior})\mathbf{Q}_{variances}. \quad (6.6)$$

$$\mathbf{E}_{posterior} = \mathbf{E}_{prior} + \tau \mathbf{C}_{prior}\mathbf{P}^T_{returns}(\mathbf{Q}_{returns}$$
$$- \mathbf{P}_{returns}\mathbf{E}_{prior}). \quad (6.7)$$

$$\mathbf{C}_{posterior} = \mathbf{C}_{prior} + \tau \mathbf{C}_{prior}\mathbf{P}^T_{covariances}(\mathbf{Q}_{covariances}$$
$$- \mathbf{P}_{covariances}\mathbf{C}_{prior}\mathbf{P}^T_{covariances}). \quad (6.8)$$

Let us look at a concrete example. We will use OBL to tell us which among three securities we should buy, sell, or stay neutral on relative to our benchmark. Our only constraint is that the buys equal sells. Thus, in this example, we will have one buy, one sell, and one neutral position. The inputs to our model are listed in Table 6.2. Note that the views expressed in the $\mathbf{Q}$ matrices in Table 6.2 are in the form

Table 6.2. Ordinal Black–Litterman Example Inputs.

Assets: [A, B, C],
w: [0.05, 0.03, 0.03],
h: [0.06, 0.07, 0.05],
$\mathbf{C}_{prior}$:
$$\begin{bmatrix} 0.060 & 0.030 & 0.020 \\ 0.030 & 0.050 & 0.025 \\ 0.02 & 0.025 & 0.040 \end{bmatrix},$$
$\mathbf{E}_{prior} = [w_1 h_1, w_2 h_2, w_3 h_3]$,
$\mathbf{P}_{variances} = [0, 1, 0]$
$\mathbf{P}_{returns} = [0, 0, 1]$
$\mathbf{P}_{covariances} = [0, 0, 1]$
$\mathbf{Q}_{variances} = [0.500, 0.333, 0.167]$,
$\mathbf{Q}_{returns} = [0.167, 0.500, 0.333]$,
$\mathbf{Q}_{covariances} = [0.500, 0.167, 0.333]$.

of relative weights indicating the strength of a view pertaining to a particular asset.

We run an optimization using sequential quadratic programming[6] to determine which securities to buy and sell. The optimization is constrained by a total allocation budget of 1% and a requirement that the sum of buys and sells must equal zero. Running the optimization tells us to sell asset A (−1%), stay neutral on asset B (0%), and buy asset C (1%).

This example is a simple one but illustrates that OBL represents a relatively straightforward adaptation of the original BL framework. Adding additional variables, constraints, and dimensions (e.g., more precise trade sizing) to the basic framework we have presented is of course possible and likely necessary in actual portfolio management applications.

6.4 Robust Optimization

In MVO, one of the critical assumptions is that the asset returns, variances, and covariances are known with certainty. Investment

---

[6]See Nocedal and Wright (2006) for formal details on sequential quadratic programming.

analysts have historically rarely questioned this assumption, believing that covariances, for example, are fairly stable over time and that MVO is relatively insensitive to the covariance assumption altogether.[7] Parameter uncertainty is real, however, and introduces the potential for model misspecification.

For some time now, there has been a drive to extend the static maxmin expected utility theory of Gilboa and Schmeidler (1989) to a dynamic environment that can be fruitfully exploited in various areas of finance, including portfolio theory. Gilboa and Schmeidler's theory provides an elegant framework for modeling decision-making that incorporates investors' aversion to uncertainty and ambiguity in the sense described by Ellsberg (1961).

For example, Fabozzi et al. (2007) showed how to apply robust portfolio optimization to MVO. In the original MVO model, the portfolio manager would include a vector of expected returns $E(r)$. In the modified version, the optimization includes a set of vectors that comprise possible expected returns $\widehat{E(r)}$. The modification represents a robust approach to optimization because it can be used to optimize to "worst-case scenarios." Those assets whose return estimations have a large amount of estimation error or variance will receive a lower portfolio weight. The following formula shows how to account for estimation errors in the MVO framework in the manner described:

$$\text{Argmax}_w \widehat{E(r)}' w - \delta' \psi - \lambda w' \Sigma w, \quad \text{with } w'l = 1, \qquad (6.9)$$

where δ is the estimation error of expected returns, ψ is a $(1 \times n)$ vector that captures the weights that react to estimation errors, w is the $(n \times 1)$ vector of portfolio allocation weights, Σ is the variance–covariance matrix of factor returns, and l is a vector of ones.

Note that the term $-\delta' \psi$ decreases the optimization function. This is not surprising as the model searches for weights that are adjusted by the estimation error of expected returns. Put differently, the robust optimization model decreases (or "shrinks") the weights of assets with large estimation errors and thus decreases the maximized expected return of the overall portfolio.

Another example of robust portfolio optimization is that provided by Simonian and Davis (2011), who extended the work on robust portfolio theory developed by Garlappi et al. (2007) and applied it to

---

[7] See, for example, Best and Grauer (1991, 1992) and Chopra and Ziemba (1993).

the BL model. The model they presented accommodates uncertainty through the use of multiple priors (in the manner of Hansen and Sargent, 2001).[8] Their robust Black–Litterman (rBL) approach is motivated by a desire to design an asset allocation framework based on the BL methodology that directly incorporates uncertainty about the covariance matrix Σ in a simple yet coherent manner.

rBL assumes that we can describe the uncertainty about Σ using a distribution derived via a bootstrap or asymptotic approximation to the sampling distribution of the covariance matrix estimator. Based on the BL methodology, there exists a systematic correspondence between each covariance matrix and the resulting BL-derived posterior distribution. In the rBL model, we begin by characterizing a neighborhood of alternative prior distributions that are also likely based on the sampling distribution of the covariance matrix Σ.

One measure that captures the relative log-likelihood of one distribution Q conditional on another distribution P is given by the Kullback–Leibler (KL) divergence measure:

$$D(P|Q) = \int_{-\infty}^{\infty} \log\left(\frac{p(x)}{q(x)}\right) p(x) \mathrm{d}x \qquad (6.10)$$

KL is a measure of the distance between two probability distributions. It is an information theoretic concept that compares the entropy of two distributions over the same random variable. The normal distribution p is compared to an approximating model, denoted by q. $D(P|Q)$ represents the information lost when one uses the model q to approximate p. Conditional on the reference prior distribution, here given by a multivariate normal with parameters μ_0 and Σ, we can calculate the expected relative log-likelihood of an alternative multivariate normal with parameters μ_a and Σ_a in closed form as

$$D(N_a|N) = \frac{1}{2}\left(\ln\left(\frac{|\Sigma_a|}{|\Sigma|}\right) + tr\left(\sum_a \sum\right)^{-1} + (\mu_a - \mu_0) - n\right), \qquad (6.11)$$

---

[8]Examples of the wide variety of applications of robust methods in finance include Hansen and Sargent (2001, 2008), Garlappi et al. (2007), Fabozzi et al. (2007), Simonian and Davis (2010, 2011), and Simonian (2011).

where we require the alternative prior distribution to be consistent with the benchmark by requiring the following additional constraint to hold:

$$\mu_a = \gamma \sum_a w_0. \quad (6.12)$$

The distribution of this statistic can be found empirically by repeatedly drawing from the sampling distribution of Σ.

rBL also introduces an additional parameter to describe the confidence the portfolio manager has in his or her estimate of the covariance matrix, similar to the concept behind the BL parameter τ that scales the portfolio manager's confidence in his or her views. We define the hyperparameter p to be the portfolio manager's confidence in the estimate of the covariance matrix, which in turn implicitly defines a value η that will be used in the rBL model. This is given by the function

$$P(D(N_a|N) \leq \eta) = 1 - p. \quad (6.13)$$

Thus, the portfolio manager's confidence level determines a neighborhood of alternative prior distributions that is a direct function of the sampling error of the covariance estimator. As the portfolio manager loses confidence in the quality of the covariance matrix estimate, the space of priors determined to be "*ex ante* plausible" expands.

Acknowledging the potential imprecision of parameter estimates alters the portfolio allocation process by imposing two constraints on the mean–variance objective function. The first constraint stipulates that the mean excess return and covariance parameters for each asset must lie within a specified confidence interval of their estimated value. This constraint implies that the investor explicitly recognizes the possibility of model misspecification. The second constraint is that a minimization over the choice of mean excess returns and covariances must be performed. The two constraints effectively transform the mean–variance objective function into a maxmin utility function, where the portfolio manager selects a probability distribution that maximizes utility while "nature" simultaneously selects a probability distribution that minimizes utility.[9] The modified utility

---

[9] See Gilboa and Schmeidler (1989).

function can be formalized as

$$\max_{w}\left\{\min_{\tilde{\Sigma}_a} w'\mu_a - \frac{\gamma}{2}w'\tilde{\Sigma}_a w\right\}, \qquad (6.14)$$

subject to the following constraint on the KL divergence of the alternative prior from the reference prior:

$$D(N_a|N) = \frac{1}{2}\left(\ln\left(\frac{|\Sigma_a|}{|\Sigma|}\right) + tr\left(\sum_a \Sigma\right)^{-1} + (\mu_a - \mu_0) - n\right) \leq \eta \qquad (6.15)$$

where the following BL relationships hold:

$$\tilde{\mu} = \mu_a + \tau \sum_a C[\tau[C' \sum_a C] + \Omega_a]^{-1}[M - C'\mu_a],$$

$$\tilde{\Sigma}_a = \Sigma_a + \left(\frac{\Sigma_a^{-1}}{\tau} + C'\Sigma_a C\right)^{-1}$$

$$\Omega = \tau \times \mathrm{diag}(C'\Sigma_a C)$$

$$\mu_a = \gamma \sum_a w_0. \qquad (6.16)$$

The end result is that the perturbed prior alters the entire BL process. Through rBL, the pivotal role of the covariance matrix in portfolio selection is brought to the fore within the framework of a Bayesian formalism that explicitly incorporates the uncertainty that investors often have in their capital market assumptions.

6.4.1 *Robust Optimization Using Machine Learning*

The robust optimization frameworks described in the previous section assume a particular distribution, i.e., are parametric, and thus have a specific range of alternative scenarios they can generate. While this does not typically diminish their utility in a significant manner, it is often the case that we would like to test our portfolios in more "exotic" scenarios so that we can gain insight into the durability of our investment strategies in the face of unforeseen and extreme market developments. As such, non-parametric approaches, such as those provided by machine learning, may be used to complement more traditional robust optimization techniques.

One possible approach is to use Generative Adversarial Networks (GANs) (Goodfellow *et al.*, 2014). GANs are a type of machine learning architecture that consists of two neural networks, the *Generator*, and the *Discriminator*, which are engaged in a minimax game. The Generator network takes random noise as input and transforms it into data, like images or time series. At the beginning of the game, its output is random and does not resemble the actual data we want to generate. Over multiple rounds (called *epochs*), the goal of the Generator is to learn how to produce data that are indistinguishable from the real data. The Discriminator network, on the other hand, takes in both real data and data created by the Generator. It tries to correctly classify whether the given data are real or fake. In the initial epochs, the synthetic data created by the Generator are quite different from the data it is trying to reproduce, while the data generated in later epochs are much closer to the original data. Thus, when the algorithm terminates, we are left with a set of synthetic data, with some elements of the set more closely resembling the original data compared to other elements in the set. For example, in the case of time series, in each epoch, a new time series will be created. When the algorithm terminates, the set of time series created will range from those that strongly parallel the original time series to those that scarcely resemble it.[10] The different time series produced thus allow investors to determine the robustness of their strategies by testing them in a variety of alternate market histories. As we will show below, we can use the GAN-generated time series as inputs for robust portfolio optimization.

Let us first take a moment to discuss GANs in more detail. The key idea behind GANs is the adversarial process. The Generator and Discriminator are in a competition. For example, imagine a case where a counterfeiter (Generator) wants to create fake artwork that looks like a real masterpiece. On the other side, you have a detective (Discriminator) whose job is to tell whether a piece of art is genuine

---

[10]For further details on using GANs to create various types of synthetic time series, see Pardo and López (2020), Papenbrock *et al.* (2021), Pardo *et al.* (2022), and Simonian (2024).

or fake. The Generator wants to create visual data that are so realistic that the Discriminator cannot tell them apart from real artwork. The Discriminator, in turn, wants to become better at distinguishing real data from fake data.

The training process involves alternating between training the Generator and training the Discriminator.[11] The Generator starts by creating random data. However, over time, the Generator tries to improve its skills by looking at the Discriminator's feedback and refining the synthetic data it produces. The Discriminator, in turn, becomes better at catching fakes. This back and forth continues through successive epochs as the Generator gets better at creating realistic data and the Discriminator gets better at detecting fake data. If the algorithm is successful, the synthetic data created by the Generator eventually become indistinguishable from real data and the Generator can be used on its own to generate new data that resemble the training data. We formally describe the GAN algorithm in Table 6.3.

When using GANs to generate adversarial scenarios for robust portfolio optimization, our objective is to identify optimal portfolio weights that perform consistently well across diverse market scenarios. The GAN-based methodology is employed to simulate a multitude of distinct time series, enabling robust optimization under uncertainty. By selecting portfolio weights that perform well across a broad spectrum of generated synthetic datasets, we can examine various performance measures (e.g., Sharpe ratio, maximum drawdown) and identify which portfolio allocation is more likely to maintain stability and favorable performance in a range of market situations.

Just as in the case of image generation, in our application of GANs to robust optimization, we attempt to recreate the original time series corresponding to the various asset classes in our portfolio. As the GAN proceeds through each epoch, it creates synthetic time series that differ from the original in varying degrees. These varied time series, which can be considered alternative market histories, can help portfolio managers build optimal portfolios that are robust across a multitude of possible market eventualities.

---

[11] The neural networks in the GAN in our example are trained using the Adam optimizer. See Kingma and Ba (2015) for more details.

Portfolio Construction

Table 6.3. GAN Algorithm.

Consider a generator G and a discriminator D engaged in a minimax game. Let z be a latent variable sampled from $p_z(z)$ and x be a data sample from an unknown distribution $p_{\text{data}}(x)$. The generator G maps z to a generated sample x, parametrized by θ_g. The discriminator D computes $D(x; \theta_d)$, indicating the probability that x is genuine. Both networks have parameters θ_g and θ_d.

Train the algorithm by iteratively updating G and D until convergence as follows:

Inputs: Data samples x from $p_{\text{data}}(x)$, latent samples z from $p_z(z)$, learning rates α_g and α_d, and hyperparameters k and n.

Step 1: Randomly initialize θ_g and θ_d.

Step 2: Update Discriminator: For k steps:

Create a sample of real data x from $p_{\text{data}}(x)$.

Create a sample of latent variables from $p_z(z)$.

Compute Discriminator loss:

$\mathcal{L}_d = \frac{1}{k} \sum_{i=1}^{k} [\log D(x_i; \theta_d) + \log(1 - D(G(z_i; \theta_g); \theta_d))]$.

Update θ_d using gradient ascent: $\theta_d \leftarrow \theta_d + \alpha_d \cdot \nabla_{\theta_d} \mathcal{L}_d$.

Step 3: Update Generator: For n steps:

Create a sample of latent variables from $p_z(z)$.

Compute Generator loss:

$\mathcal{L}_g = -\frac{1}{n} \sum_{i=1}^{n} \log D(G(z_i; \theta_g); \theta_d)$.

Update θ_g using gradient ascent: $\theta_g \leftarrow \theta_g + \alpha_g \cdot \nabla_{\theta_g} \mathcal{L}_g$.

We describe the GAN-driven robust optimization process formally in Table 6.4.

The approach described in Table 6.4 yields a set of portfolio weights that perform consistently well across diverse market scenarios. The incorporation of GAN-generated adversarial scenarios, asset volatilities, and correlations enhances the robustness of the portfolio optimization process, enabling better risk-adjusted returns under model uncertainty. Let us illustrate this framework with an example. Suppose we have a portfolio consisting of five assets, with model inputs listed in Table 6.5. We assume that the historical time series used to derive the values in Table 6.5 are available for analysis and processing.

Table 6.4. GAN Algorithm for Robust Portfolio Optimization.

Let N denote the number of assets in the portfolio.

μ represents the vector of initial return estimates for N assets.

Σ represents the initial covariance matrix for N assets.

Let K denote the input size for the GAN.

$K = N + \frac{N(N+1)}{2}$,

where $\frac{N(N+1)}{2}$ refers to the lower triangular elements of the covariance matrix.

GAN Hyperparameters:

$\alpha = 0.001$ is the learning rate for the optimizer.

$T = 1000$ is the number of training epochs.

$M = 200$ is the desired number of generated adversarial scenarios.

Generator Model:

Define G as the Generator in the GAN. G maps an input vector x of size K to synthetic portfolio scenarios and consists of two linear transformations followed by Rectified Linear Unit (ReLU) activation:

$z_1 = \text{ReLU}(W_1 \cdot x + b_1)$,

$z_2 = W_2 \cdot z_1 + b_2$,

where W_1, W_2, b_1, and b_2 are learnable parameters.

GAN Initialization:

(1) Initialize the Generator G with random weights and biases.
(2) Use the optimizer to update the parameters of G with learning rate α.

GAN Training Loop:

For each training epoch t from 1 to T:

(1) Generate M synthetic portfolio scenarios using G and random noise.
(2) Ensure that the shape of the generated scenarios matches the input size K.
(3) Split the generated data into:
   (i) Expected returns: R_{gen}, an $M \times N$ matrix.
   (ii) Lower triangular covariance matrix elements: L_{gen}, an $M \times \frac{N(N+1)}{2}$ matrix.

(*Continued*)

Table 6.4. (*Continued*)

(4) Define the loss function for training the GAN. The loss consists of two terms:
   (i) Expected returns term: $\text{Loss}_1 = \frac{1}{M} \sum_{i=1}^{M} \|R_{\text{gen}}^i - \mu\|^2$.
   (ii) Covariance matrix term: $\text{Loss}_2 = \frac{1}{M} \sum_{i=1}^{M} \|\Sigma_{\text{gen}}^i - \Sigma\|$.
   (iii) The total loss is the sum of Loss_1 and Loss_2.
   (iv) Update the parameters of G using backpropagation and optimization to minimize the total loss.

Calculation of Portfolio Weights:

Identify the optimal portfolio weights w_{opt} by selecting the weight set that maximizes the portfolio's Sharpe ratio. Normalize the weights as necessary to ensure they sum up to 1.

Table 6.5. Inputs to Robust GAN Portfolio Optimization.

Number of epochs: 1000

GAN learning rate: 0.001

Number of adversarial scenarios: 200

Reference Asset returns: [8%, 12%, 10%, 9%, 11%]

Reference Asset covariance matrix:
$$\begin{bmatrix} 0.010 & 0.005 & 0.004 & 0.002 & 0.003 \\ 0.005 & 0.020 & 0.015 & 0.008 & 0.010 \\ 0.004 & 0.015 & 0.030 & 0.010 & 0.012 \\ 0.002 & 0.008 & 0.010 & 0.015 & 0.007 \\ 0.003 & 0.010 & 0.012 & 0.007 & 0.025 \end{bmatrix}.$$

Our only constraints are that the portfolio's individual asset weights sum to one ("no leverage") and that the assets in the portfolio must each have weights equal to or greater than zero ("no shorting"). Running our optimization, we get the following set of portfolio weights: [0.1593, 0.2392, 0.2008, 0.1792, 0.2215]. It is noteworthy that even with a minimal set of constraints, we have a portfolio that is well diversified. This can be considered a residual benefit of the process.

6.5 Judgment Aggregation

In most portfolio construction models, it is implicitly assumed that it is a single view that is being expressed. However, in actual portfolio management practice, investment decisions are often made by a team of portfolio managers. In a more informal investment process, collective decision-making is not very challenging from a technical standpoint. As long as an acceptable deliberation process is available to the team, decision-making generally proceeds without major impediments. However, aggregating portfolio manager judgments using a quantitative process can present complications given the requirement that the aggregated judgments must typically conform to some mathematical standards of consistency and coherence.

The most natural way for investors to express their investment views is via probabilities. However, the challenge in combining disparate probability estimates in the form of individual posterior estimates is that, in aggregating them, care must be taken to ensure that they are based on the same set of considerations and, in turn, that the aggregate is probabilistically coherent, with coherence defined as being consistent with Kolmogorov's (1956) axioms and any rules that they imply. The problem of aggregating probability estimates is formally related to the problem of judgment aggregation, which in turn is an extension of the preference aggregation problem studied by Kenneth Arrow (1951). In the domain of judgment aggregation, the premises that support a decision are as much an object of study as the decisions themselves. In cases involving deductive reasoning, of particular interest are those where the majority of a given collective agrees on a conclusion that contradicts the conclusion implied by the majority votes on each of the premises (Kornhauser and Sager 1986, Pettit, 2001). Solutions to this problem are typically evaluated based on their providing a credible case that the solution presents a genuine rational collective decision, with the collective held to plausible standards of rationality and fairness.

As an example, consider the following judgment aggregation problem: The employee-owners of a company are considering taking a pay cut in order to provide funds for a safety measure to guard against electrocution. In deciding whether or not to forgo the funds they would otherwise save, they are to consider two issues: (1) whether there is sufficient danger of electrocution to merit a safety measure

Table 6.6. Judgment Aggregation Problem.

Worker	Serious Danger?	Effective measure?	Pay sacrifice?
1	Yes	No	No
2	No	Yes	No
3	Yes	Yes	Yes

and (2) whether the safety measure in question is judged to be effective. They are to vote Yes for a pay sacrifice if and only if they vote Yes for both (1) and (2). This scenario is depicted in tabular form in Table 6.6.

As we see in Table 6.6, the conclusion implied by the majority vote on each of the premises, "Yes," is inconsistent with the majority vote on the conclusion, "No." In response to this dilemma, various solutions have been proposed that aim to resolve the inconsistency formally as well as provide plausible pictures of collective rationality (List and Pettit (2002), List (2003), Pigozzi (2005, 2006).

The type of problem shown in Table 6.6 is a bi-conditional (i.e., of the form $(x \wedge y) \leftrightarrow z$) and thus exemplifies deductive reasoning where conclusions are derived from premises according to the rules of propositional logic. In contrast to the deductive model presented here, decision-making in finance usually employs inductive reasoning, namely, probabilistic reasoning. Any mechanism that aggregates disparate probabilistic views must thus produce results that are probabilistically coherent.

For example, let us assume that a team consisting of two portfolio managers is in the process of forming a joint view a on an asset class x based on a consideration of future GDP growth and how it bears on a. For our purposes here, it is not important what the specific view of each manager is. However, the managers must base their decision on the probability p that their view a will be correct, *given* the probability q that a particular economic regime materializes in the coming quarter (e.g., high GDP, low inflation).

Let us suppose that each of our managers has assigned a probability to $p|q$ based on an assessment of the propositions q and $p \wedge q$ in the manner shown in Table 6.7.

Assuming we give equal weight to each portfolio manager's probability assignments, the *prima facie* fairest way to generate a genuinely

Table 6.7. Hypothetical Portfolio Manager Probability Assignments.

Manager	q	$p \wedge q$	$p\mid q$
1	0.50	0.10	0.20
2	0.25	0.20	0.80

collective opinion is to take the average of the values that each manager posits for each proposition. However, averaging does not work in this case because the average value that the proposition $p\mid q$ takes, 0.50, is probabilistically incoherent given that $\frac{p \wedge q}{q} = \frac{0.15}{0.375} = 0.40$. Given the prevalence of this type of outcome, a more nuanced method of generating a coherent aggregation of probabilistic opinions is needed. Osherson and Vardi (2006), for example, offered an optimization-based solution to such cases that locates the minimum distance, defined as absolute deviation, between sets of individual opinions by means of simulated annealing. Here, we show how the Shapely value (SV) discussed in Chapter 3 can also be used to generate coherent aggregations of probability estimates.[12] As we shall see, the SV not only provides a formal solution to the problem of probabilistic coherence but also provides an outcome that can genuinely be viewed as a *cooperative* solution.

Recall from Chapter 3 the axioms that serve as the basis for the SV. In the present context, a direct application of the efficiency axiom $\left(\sum_{i \in N} \phi_i(v) = v(N)\right)$ is not possible, as our goal is not the fair allocation of resources, but the coherent allocation of probability estimates. As such, we replace the foregoing axiom with the following alternative axiom:

$$\text{Consistency:} \ \forall R, \mathbf{CON}R. \qquad (6.17)$$

Axiom (6.17) states that on any given ordering, the consistency of the order with the Kolmogorov axioms must be preserved. The consistency axiom will thus, on every order, force certain propositions to take on specific values so that they maintain consistency with the values assigned to the propositions preceding them. Conceptually,

---

[12] This section is based on Simonian (2012) and Simonian (2014).

(6.17) shares the same motivation as axioms that are used to build games with restricted coalitions and permission games, such as those described in Gilles, Owen, and van den Brink (1992) and Derks and Peters (1993). In the framework presented here, where interconnected propositions are the players in a game, the propositions in a given order that precede the final proposition are analogous to players with veto or other regulatory powers in standard permission games because they possess the ability to determine what value the final proposition takes based on their position in the order.

In some situations, it is desirable to abandon the symmetry axiom ($v(S \cup \{i\}) = v(S \cup \{j\})$, for every S of N) as well and allow different weightings for the players in order to imbue them with more or less influence over the final outcome of deliberation. In the present context, this will be the case when one wishes to assign different levels of importance to each portfolio manager, perhaps due to differing levels of expertise, seniority, etc. Kalai and Samet (1987) provided an overview of ways to augment the SV solution using different weighting schemes. In addition to weighting, we note that other variations of the SV are possible, some of which depart from the procedure of simple averaging across uniform orderings (for an overview, see Monderer and Samet, 2002). One variation is the *quasivalue*, in which the SV solution is a random order value but, unlike the original SV solution, the random orders are not uniformly drawn. Yet another departure from the original SV solution changes the domain over which the solution is defined. Thus, rather than assuming a *grand coalition* N among a set of players, it is assumed that there is a fixed partition of N, a *coalitional structure*, such that each coalition serves as the basic unit of allocation. In our example in the next section, we consider a weighted version of the SV.

6.5.1 *Forming Collective Views*

In applying the SV to aggregating disparate probability estimates, the problem we encounter is not one where participants are trying to gain a larger share of a resource or determine fair distribution costs for a joint project, but one where individuals are attempting to have their views expressed to the fullest extent possible while simultaneously maintaining cohesion as a genuine collective entity. Their goal is to have a fair representation of each individual's opinion within one collective opinion. In a sense, the goal is to arrive at a coherent and fair allocation of "epistemic influence."

Although the method that seems fairest at first blush, averaging, usually results in incoherent outcomes, it is nevertheless reasonable to assume that the estimates resulting from averaging the opinions of each portfolio manager represent their *ideal values*, in the same way that each individual's claim of a share of a finite resource represents the ideal value for that individual in the original SV. Again, under this interpretation of the problem, the players in the game are the propositions being considered, not the individual portfolio managers. Thus, the problem in cases of probabilistic opinion aggregation is to derive a collective opinion that gets as close to the average opinion as possible *given* the requirement that the pattern of reasoning contained in the solution be probabilistically coherent.

To see how our epistemic version of the SV is applied in practice, let us return to our previous example of the two portfolio managers, where the ideal (average) values for propositions q, $p \wedge q$, and $p|q$ are 0.375, 0.15, and 0.50, respectively. In Table 6.8, we display the orderings for the set of propositions as called for by Shapley's solution. For notational convenience, we identify the propositions q, $p \wedge q$, $p|q$ with the labels x, y, and z, respectively. On the initial ordering, xyz, the value for x is posited first. Because it is posited first, the average value for x, 0.375, is assigned. The second proposition in the order, y, is also allowed to take on its ideal value of 0.15. The third proposition in the order, however, z, is not allowed to take on its ideal value because doing so would render the set of propositions probabilistically incoherent. Thus, it is forced to take on the value of 0.40. As we proceed to calculate the SV for all orderings, we see that the final assignment of probability estimates is coherent as well.

We note that the end result in Table 6.8 is coherent to the second decimal place. At the third decimal, we will find that $q/p \wedge q = 0.464$, while the SV estimate for $p|q = 0.466$. Depending on how precise we require our estimates to be, we can iterate the foregoing procedure using our initial SV estimates to generate more coherent sets of estimates. For example, if we take the SVs in Table 6.8 as our ideal values and repeat our solution procedure, we generate the result in Table 6.9.

Portfolio Construction

Table 6.8. Epistemic Shapley Orderings.

Ordering	x	y	z
xyz	0.375	0.15	0.40
xzy	0.375	0.1875	0.50
yxz	0.375	0.15	0.40
yzx	0.30	0.15	0.50
zxy	0.375	0.1875	0.50
zyx	0.30	0.15	0.50
SV	0.35	0.1625	0.46

Table 6.9. Epistemic Shapley Orderings II.

Ordering	x	y	z
xyz	0.35	0.1625	0.464
xzy	0.35	0.16333	0.466
yxz	0.35	0.1625	0.464
yzx	0.348	0.1625	0.466
zxy	0.35	0.1633	0.466
zyx	0.348	0.1625	0.466
SV	0.349	0.1627	0.465

The estimate for $q/p \wedge q = 0.465872$, while the SV estimate for $p|q = 0.465873$. Each iteration can thus be characterized as providing a "coherence adjustment" over each previous iteration.

Finally, we can use the foregoing procedure to accommodate a weighted variant of the SV as well. However, in contrast to the approaches described by Kalai and Samet, we treat weighting directly by adjusting the ideal values for each estimate to reflect the importance assigned to each portfolio manager. Suppose, for example, that the opinion of Manager 1 is twice as valuable as the opinion of Manager 2. Accordingly, we assign Manager 1's opinions a weight of 0.666 and assign Manager 2's opinions a weight of 0.334. Given this weighting scheme, we calculate weighted sums for each of the propositions by multiplying each manager's respective weight by their probability assignment. Doing so produces the following weighted ideal values: $q = 0.4165$, $p \wedge q = 0.1334$, $p|q = 0.4004$. In Table 6.10, we show our weighted orderings. As in the case with symmetric weighting, the coherence of the result in Table 6.10 can be refined via iteration.

Table 6.10. Weighted Epistemic Shapley Orderings.

Ordering	x	y	z
xyz	0.4165	0.1334	0.32
xzy	0.4165	0.1668	0.4004
yxz	0.4165	0.1334	0.32
yzx	0.3331	0.1334	0.4004
zxy	0.4165	0.1668	0.4004
zyx	0.3331	0.1334	0.4004
SV	0.3887	0.1445	0.372

6.6 Concluding Points

This book has presented an approach to geopolitical analysis that draws on game theory, machine learning, and causal inference. The intent was to give investors the formal tools to conduct rigorous analyses of geopolitical interaction, in order to develop well-founded inputs into macro-driven portfolios. While forming robust investment views is a critical aspect of portfolio management, it is also imperative to have a structured framework for implementing investment views in a portfolio. To that end, in this chapter, we have discussed several portfolio construction and optimization techniques that give investors the ability to translate their geopolitical and macro views into concrete portfolio positions. Well-known portfolio selection approaches using linear programming, mean–variance optimization, and the Black–Litterman model were discussed. Further, we provided a detailed overview of robust approaches to portfolio construction, which try to account for model misspecification. We presented traditional frameworks for robust optimization, as well as a novel approach to robust portfolio selection based on Generative Adversarial Networks. Finally, because portfolio decisions are often made in teams, we presented an original game theoretic approach to complex judgment aggregation using the Shapley value.

References

Arrow, K. 1951. *Social Choice and Individual Values*. New York: Wiley.
Black, F. and Litterman, R.B. 1990. Asset allocation: Combining investor views with market equilibrium. *Technical Report, Goldman Sachs & Co.*

Black, F. and Litterman, R.B. 1991. Global asset allocation with equities, bonds and currencies. *Technical report, Goldman Sachs & Co.*

Black, F. and Litterman, R. 1992. Global portfolio optimization. *Financial Analysts Journal* 48(5): 28–43.

Derks, J. and Peters, H. 1993. A shapley value for games with restricted coalitions. *International Journal of Game Theory* 21(4): 351–360.

Ellsberg, D. 1961. Risk, ambiguity, and the savage axioms. *The Quarterly Journal of Economics* 75(4): 643–669.

Fabozzi, F.J., Kolm, P.N., Pachamanova, D.A. and Focardi, S.M. 2007. *Robust Portfolio Optimization and Management*. Hoboken, NJ: John Wiley & Sons.

Garlappi, L., Uppal, R. and Wang, T. 2007. Portfolio selection with parameter and model uncertainty: A multi-prior approach. *The Review of Financial Studies* 20(1): 41–81.

Gilboa, I. and Schmeidler, D. 1989. Maxmin expected utility with a non-unique Prior. *Journal of Mathematical Economics* 18(2): 141–153.

Gilles, R.P., Owens, G. and van den Brink, R. 1992. Games with permission structures: The conjunctive approach. *International Journal of Game Theory* 20(3): 277–293.

Goodfellow, I.J., Pouget-Abadie, J., Mirza, M., Xu, B., Warde-Farley, D., Ozair, S., Courville, A. and Bengio, Y. 2014. Generative Adversarial Nets. *Proceedings of the 27th International Conference on Neural Information Processing Systems* 2: 2672–2680.

Hansen, L.P. and Sargent, T.J. 2001. "Robust Control and Model Uncertainty." *American Economic Review* 91(2): 60–66.

Hansen, L.P. and Sargent, T.J. 2008. *Robustness*. Princeton, NJ: Princeton University Press.

Kalai, E. and Samet, D. 1987. On weighted shapley values. *International Journal of Game Theory* 16(3): 205–222.

Karmarkar, N. 1984. A new polynomial-time algorithm for linear programming. *Proceedings of the Sixteenth Annual ACM Symposium on Theory of Computing*, 302–311.

Khachiyan, L.G. 1979. "A Polynomial Algorithm in Linear Programming." *Soviet Mathematics Doklady* 20: 191–194.

Kingma, D. and Ba, J. 2015. Adam: A method for stochastic optimization. *Proceedings of the 3rd International Conference on Learning Representations (ICLR 2015)*.

Kolm, P.N., Ritter, G. and Simonian, J. 2021. Black–litterman and beyond: The bayesian paradigm in investment management. *Journal of Portfolio Management* 47(5): 91–113.

Kolmogorov, A. 1956. *Foundations of the Theory of Probability*, 2nd edition, New York: Chelsea.

Kornhauser, L.A. and Sager, L.G. 1986. Unpacking the court. *Yale Law Journal* 96(1): 82–117.

List, C. and Pettit, P. 2002. Aggregating sets of judgments: An impossibility result. *Economics and Philosophy* 18(1): 89–110.

List, C. 2003. A possibility theorem on aggregation over multiple interconnected propositions. *Mathematical Social Sciences* 45(1):1–13.

Markowitz, H. 1952. Portfolio selection. *The Journal of Finance* 7(1): 77–91.

Monderer, D. and Samet, D. 2002. Variations on the shapley value. In *Handbook of Game Theory No. III*, Aumann, R.J. and Hart, S. (eds.), 2055–2076. Amsterdam: Elsevier Science.

Nocedal, J. and Wright, S.J. 2006. *Numerical Optimization*. Springer.

Osherson, D.N. and Vardi, M.Y. 2006. Aggregating disparate estimates of chance. *Games and Economic Behavior* 56(1): 148–173.

Papenbrock, J., Schwendner, P., Jaeger, M. and Krügel, S. 2021. Matrix evolutions: Synthetic correlations and explainable machine learning for constructing robust investment portfolios. *The Journal of Financial Data Science* 3(2): 51–69.

Pardo, F.D. and López, R.C. 2020. Mitigating overfitting on financial datasets with generative adversarial networks. *The Journal of Financial Data Science* 2(1): 76–85.

Pardo, F.D., Schwendner, P. and Wunsch, M. 2022. Tackling the exponential scaling of signature-based generative adversarial networks for high-dimensional financial time-series generation. *The Journal of Financial Data Science* 4(4): 110–132.

Pettit, P. 2001. Deliberative democracy and the discursive dilemma. *Philosophical Issues* 11(1): 268–299.

Pigozzi, G. 2006. Belief merging and the discursive dilemma: An argument-based account to paradoxes of judgment aggregation. *Synthese* 152(2): 285–298.

Pigozzi, G. 2005. Two aggregation paradoxes in social decision making: The ostrogorski paradox and the discursive dilemma. *Episteme: A Journal of Individual and Social Epistemology* 2(2): 33–42.

Simonian, J. and Davis, J. 2010. Robust value-at-risk: An information-theoretic approach. *Applied Economics Letters* 17 (16): 1551–1553.

Simonian, J. and Davis, J. 2011. Incorporating uncertainty into the black–litterman portfolio selection model. *Applied Economics Letters* 18(17): 1719–1722.

Simonian, J. 2012. A formal methodology for aggregating multiple market views. *Applied Financial Economics* 22(14): 1175–1179.

Simonian, J. 2014. Copula-opinion pooling with complex opinions. *Quantitative Finance* 14(6): 941–946.

Simonian, J. 2024. Investment Model Validation: A Guide for Practitioners. CFA Research Foundation.

Index

A

active management, 136
aggregating multiple investor views, 130
agreements, 59
alliance formation, 62–63
allocation of resources, 60
altruism, 31–32, 51
Andras, P., 50
Angrist, J.D., 99
Arrow, Kenneth, 148
artificial intelligence, 111
assurance, 54
assurance problem, 53
Attack–Defense game, 35
Aumann, R., 67
average treatment effect, 101
Axelrod, R., 27–28, 37
Azerbaijan, 20

B

Ba, J., 144
backdoor adjustment, 105
bacteria, 50
Bareinboim, E., 106
bargaining power, 65–66
Barto, A.G., 107
battle of the sexes game, 48–49, 107, 109

Bayesian, 107–108, 119, 135, 142
Bayesian game, 38–40, 45, 88
Bayesian network, 111
bees, 51
belief networks, 111
Bellman equation, 73
Bernheim, B.D., 12
Best and Grauer, 139
beta distribution, 108
betas, 131
biases, 129–130
Black, F., 135
Black–Litterman (BL) model, 135–136, 142, 154
blocking conditions, 122
Borel, E., 116
bounded rationality, 4, 7, 49
boundedness, 24
Brams, S.J., 116
Brexit, 53
Bshary, R., 50

C

Campbell, D.T., 96
causal analysis, 119, 121, 133
causal beliefs, 112
causal dependence, 102, 121
causal distance, 133
causal effect, 103
causal ignorance, 119

causal inference, 95, 100–102, 125, 129, 154
causal markov condition (CMC), 121
causal network, 111
causal proximity, 121
causal reinforcement learning, 106
causal relations, ix, 125
causal scenarios, 120
causal views, 132
causality, 95
causality in economics, 99
causation, 97
cause, 96
central bank, 36–37, 76, 78–79, 82–83, 85
chain, 122
characteristic function, 65
Cheney, D., 12
China, 18
Chopra and Ziemba, 139
CMAB algorithms, 45
coalition, 60–61, 65
coalitional structure, 151
coherence adjustment, 153
collective action, 14, 29, 62, 68
collective good, 31
collective opinion, 152
collective reasoning, 61
collective utility, 60
collective views, 151
collider, 122
Collingwood, R.G., 96
Colonel Blotto game, 116
commitment, 5, 14, 27, 32, 45
commodity prices, 96
common cause, 96–97
computational game theory, vii
computational global macro, vi
conditional average treatment effect (CATE), 101–102
conditional independencies, 121
conditional probability table, 111
conflict, 23
conformists, 12
confound, 101
confounder, 108–110, 116–117

confounding, 103
confounding variables, 102
Conitzer, V., 81
consequentialist, 5
constrained maximization, 5, 131
constrained maximizer, 4
constrained minimization, 133
constraints, 131, 133, 141
consumer spending, 104
context, 38, 40, 42, 55
contextual multi-armed bandit (CMAB), viii, 37–38, 40–42, 55, 71–72, 93
conventions, 14, 67–68
Cook, T.D., 96
cooperate, 58
cooperating, 60
cooperation, 7–8, 13–14, 26–29, 31–33, 49–56, 59, 62, 64, 66, 68–69
cooperative, 150
cooperative game, 47, 60, 65
coordination, 83–84
coordination games, 67
correlated equilibrium, 66–67
correlating device, 67–68
correlations, 125
counterfactual, 95, 101–102
counterfactual dependence, 121–122
counterfactual distance, 122, 124
Cowles commission, 98–99
Crandall, J.W., 38
Crimea, 18
Cruz, J.B., 81

D

Davis, J., 139–140
Dawkins, R., 51
Dayan, P., 72
de Prado, M., ix
decision-making, 69, 71, 73, 77, 79, 84, 108–109, 119, 125, 129–130, 139
deductive logic, 111
deductive reasoning, 148–149
defect, 27, 33
defection, 26, 55

defensive realism, 16
Derks, J., 151
developing countries, 17
diachronic, 2, 6, 24, 32
Díez, 112
difference-in-differences analysis, 100
directed acyclic graph, 102–104, 121–122
directed separation, 122
Dirichlet distribution, 107
discount rate, 76
discretionary global macro, v
discriminator, 143–144
do operator, 101–102
dominating strategy, 26–27
doves, 19
Dudik, M., 38

E

econometrics, 99
economic alliances, 62
economic causality, 98
economic causes, 99
economic laws, 99
economic policy, 96
economic policymaking, 96
economic processes, 99
economic theory, 98
Ellsberg, D., 139
Elster, J., 31
emerging market, 17
emotions, 129–130
entropy, 140
environmental adversity, 50
epistemic influence, 152
epistemic Shapley orderings, 153–154
epistemic utility, 132
epochs, 143, 147
Epstein, G.S., 116
equilibrium, 25, 27, 34, 82
Eshel, I., 28
ETFs, 131
EU, 18, 53, 76
European central bank (ECB), 48–49, 76, 82, 84–85

Eurozone, 82
Eva, B., 121, 124
Evader, 85–86, 88–89
evidential similarity, 121
evolutionarily, 54
evolutionarily committed cooperators, 54
evolutionary, 51
exchange rate policy, 19
expectations, 25, 28
expected payoffs, 40
expected utility, 27
exploitation, 38, 41, 73
exploiting, 72
exploration, 38, 41, 73, 93
exploring, 72
external solutions, 28, 31

F

Fabozzi, F., 99, 139
fair, 59–60
Favero, C., 99
Fed, 49, 72, 76, 82–85
federal funds, 96
federal funds rate, 82
federal reserve, 48
financial data science, 99
focal points, 67–68
follower, 81–82
FOMC, 81, 113
football, 35
foreign direct investment, 103
free-rider problem, 2–3
Frieden, J.A., 19
future payoffs, 28

G

Gale, D., 62
Gale–Shapley algorithm, viii, 62, 64
game theoretic, 24, 130, 154
game theory, vii, 23–25, 34, 129, 154
game with lexicographic beliefs, 90, 92
games of incomplete information, 38, 89

games with restricted coalitions, 151
Garlappi, L., 139–140
Gasking, D., 96
Gauthier, David, 4, 32–33
Gayane, 48
general agreement on tariffs and trade (GATT), 59
generative adversarial networks (GAN), 143, 145–147, 154
generator, 143–144
genes, 51
geopolitical analysis, 34, 45, 61, 154
geopolitical events, 93
geopolitical interaction, 36
geopolitical risk, 15, 19, 23
geopolitical views, 129, 131
geopolitics, 19, 82
Gilboa, I., 139, 141
Gilles, R.P., 151
Gittins, J.C., 38
global macro investing, v
Good, I.J., 111
Goodfellow, I.J., 143
Goodrich, M.A., 38
Gossink, D.E., 112
grand coalition, 151
Granger, C.W.J., 98–99
Granger causality, 98–99
great financial crisis, 76
gross domestic product (GDP), 103, 113, 149
Guyer, M.J., 116

H

Hansen, L.P., 140
Hasselt, H.V., 72
Hausman, D.M., 96
hawks, 19
He, 136
Heizler, O., 116
Hendry, D.F., 99
Henrion, M., 112
Hicks, J., 98
hierarchical NOR, 115
Hobbes, T., 29

Holland, 96
Homicidal Chauffeur, 86–89
homo economicus, 3
homo politicus, 3
Hong Kong, 18
Hood, W., 99
Hoover, K.D., 98–99
hospital–resident problem, 62
human development index, 103
Hume, D., 95
hyperparameter, 135

I

ideal values, 152
India, 18
individual treatment effect, 101–102
individualists, 12
individuals, 16
inductive reasoning, 149
inferential approaches to economic causality, 99
inferential process approach, 99–100
inferential structural approaches, 98
inflation, 49, 76, 79, 82–83, 85, 105, 149
information theoretic, 140
inhibiting causes, 113–114
institutions, 16
instrumental variable analysis, 100
intentions, 9
interest rate, 36–37, 49, 82–83, 104
internal and external drivers of geopolitical risk, 19
internal solutions, 28, 31
international affairs, 37, 75, 87, 93
international relations, 15
international system, 15, 82
interstate conflict, 15
interstate negotiations, 72
interstate relations, 17–18
intervention, 100–103
investment views, 129
Isaacs, R., 85
Isbell, L.A., 50
iterative game, 37–38, 40

J

Janson, C.H., 50
Japan, 76
jointness, 2
judgment aggregation, 148–149

K

Kalai, E., 151, 153
Karmarkar, N., 131
Kashmir, 18
Katehakis, M.N., 38
Keohane, R.O., 16
Khachaturian, 48
Khachiyan, L.G., 131
kin cooperation, 51
Kingma, D., 144
Kolm, P.N., 135
Kolmogorov, A., 148, 150
Koopmans, T., 99
Kornhauser, L.A., 148
Krueger, A.B., 99
Kullback–Leibler (KL) divergence, 140, 142

L

labor unions, 36
law enforcement, 85
laws, 14
Lazarus, J., 50
leader, 81–82
leak probability, 112
Lee, S., 106, 135
Lemmer, J.F., 112
Lewis, 122
lexicographic beliefs, 89–90
Li, T., 81
liberalism, 16
linear programming, 131, 134, 154
linear programming framework, 133
List, C., 149
Litterman, R.B., 135–136
López, R.C., 143

M

machine learning, vii, 130, 143, 154
macro, 154
macro views, 129
Mafia, 33
manipulation approach to causality, 96
marginal contribution, 61
market exposures, 130
Markov decision processes (MDPs), 72–73
Markov equivalence, 122
Marvell, G., 34
matching pennies, 35
maximization, 49
maximize, 24, 27, 37, 50, 82, 87
maximizing difference, 35
maxmin expected utility theory, 139
maxmin utility, 141
Maynard Smith, J., 28, 37
McGraw, 50
mean–variance optimization (MVO), 138–139, 154
Mearsheimer, J.J., 16
mental models, 15
Menzies, P., 96
middle east, 18
military engagements, 75
military operations, 85
minimax, 145
minimax game, 143
model misspecification, 141, 154
mole rats, 50
Monderer, D., 151
monetary policy, 36, 47, 49, 64, 75, 78, 83, 96
money supply, 36
moral claims, 34
moral rules, 32–33
mortar men, 29
multi-armed bandit, 69
multi-period interactions, 37
multiple equilibria, 47
multiple utility functions, 13

Mussard, S., 60
Myerson value (MV), 64–66

N

Nash equilibrium, 25, 48, 52, 67, 75
natural constants, 98
natural gas, 90
negative (inhibiting) causes, 112
negative externalities, 33
negotiation, 60, 90
net conditional probability, 112
neural networks, 143
Niranjan, M., 107
Nocedal, J., 138
Noe, R., 50
Noisy-OR (NOR), 111, 113–116, 118
non-collider, 122
non-equilibrium, 27
non-excludability, 2
non-instrumental, 24
noncooperative games, 24–45, 47, 55
norm, 9–10, 12–14, 33
normalized counterfactual distance, 124
North Korea, 20
nuclear non-proliferation treaty, 53

O

objective function, 131, 133, 141
offensive realism, 16
on-policy learning algorithm, 107
optimal action, 72
optimal decisions, 72
optimal strategies, 37, 82
optimization, 84, 132, 134, 154
orangutans, 51
ordering, 61
ordinal Black–Litterman (OBL), 136–138
orientation discovery algorithm, 122–123
Osherson, D.N., 150
Ostrom, E., 29
outcome, 102
Owens, G., 151

P

Pakistan, 18
Papenbrock, J., 143
Pardo, F.D., 143
Pareto efficient, 48
Pareto inferior, 27
Pareto optimal, 25, 27, 52
payoff, 25–26, 37, 40, 44, 54–56, 58, 60–61, 65, 71, 76, 79, 81–84, 87–88, 91–92, 109
Pearl, J., 96, 101, 111
Pearson correlations, 131
Peng, Y., 111
Perea, A., 90
permission games, 151
personal identity, 12
Peters, H., 151
Petrosyan, L., 85
Pettit, P., 148–149
Pigozzi, G., 149
players, 25
policy, 73
political stability, 103
political-military conflict, 36
portfolio allocation, 135
portfolio construction, 125, 129, 131, 154
portfolio management, 129, 148, 154
portfolio optimization, 130, 144, 147
portfolio optimization techniques, 129
positions, 86
positive (promoting), 112
positive cause, 97
positive-sum games, 68
predation, 54
preferences, 23–25, 64
Price, G.R., 37
Price, H., 96
primates, 12, 50–51
prior, 135
Prisoner's Dilemma (PD), 25–29, 31–35, 52, 54, 107, 109
probabilistic causation, 97
probabilistic coherence, 150
probabilistic dependence, 121

probabilistic independencies, 121
probabilistic reasoning, 149
probability, 150–152
probability distance, 121
promoting causes, 113–114
propensity score matching, 100
proportional navigation, 86
public good, 29, 31
punishment, 30, 37
Pursuer, 85–86, 88–89
Pursuit–Evasion game, 85–87

Q

Q-function, 73
Q-learning, ix, 69, 72, 91, 93, 107, 110
QE, 76
quadratic programming, 134

R

randomized controlled trials, 100
Rapoport, A., 116
rational, 26, 54
rationality, 3, 10, 24, 26
Rawls, 13–14
realism, 15–16
receiver, 77
Recep Tayyip Erdoğan, 16
reciprocity, 27–28
rectified linear unit, 146
Reggia, J.A., 111
regression modeling, 100
regret, 38
reinforcement learning, vii, 23, 37, 69, 72, 93, 129
relations, 1
relative payoffs, 34
reputation, 8
reservation values, 66
resource allocation, 130
resource competition, 51, 54
reward, 37, 40
risk–return, 130
risks, 130
rite of spring, 48
Robbins, H., 38

robotics, 85
robust Black–Litterman (rBL), 140–142
robust optimization, 138, 142–144, 154
robust portfolio optimization, 146
rules, 13–14
rules, habits, and conventions, 2
Rummery, G.A., 107
Run–Pass game, 35–37, 39, 41, 43–44
Russia, 18, 53

S

Sager, L.G., 148
Samet, D., 151, 153
Sandholm, T., 81
Sargent, T.J., 140
satisficers, 4
satisficing, 5, 49
Schelling, T., 67–68
Schmeidler, D., 139, 141
Schmitt, D.R., 34
Schmidhuber, J., 72
Schulman, J., 72
security alliances, 47
selection bias, 101
selective pressures, 54
self-interest, 26, 31, 51–52
Sen, A., 6
sender, 77
sensitivity analysis, 43, 85
Sethi, S.P., 81
sequential quadratic programming, 138
Seyfarth, R.M., 12
Shapley, Lloyd, 60, 62
Shapley value (SV), x, 60–61, 64, 66, 150–154
signal quality, 78–81
signaling, 79
signaling game, 77–78
Simaan, M., 81
Simon, Herbert, 4, 99
Simonian, J., vi, ix, 60, 99, 112, 120, 139–140, 150

Sims, C.A., 99
simulated annealing, 150
simulation, 40–44, 56, 58, 79, 82, 88–89, 107–108, 117
Skyrms, B., 51–52, 56
social context, 10
social environment, 13
social identities, 13
social norms, 9–10, 32, 34
social role, 11–12, 54
speed, 87
Spence, Michael, 77
spontaneous solutions, 31
Srinivas, S., 112
stable cooperative structures, 62
stable marriage, 62
Stackelberg, 81
Stackelberg game, 82, 84
Stag Hunt (SH), 52–56, 58–59
State–Action–Reward–State–Action (SARSA), 107–108, 110
state of nature, 29
states, 17, 73
strategic interaction, 45, 71
Stravinsky, 48
structural approaches, 99
structural approaches to economic causality, 98
structural causal model (SCM), 102–103
subgame, 61
Sunstein, Cass, 10, 54
Suppes, 97
Sutton, R.S., 107
synchronic, 2, 24, 32
synthetic data, 130, 143–144
systematic global macro, v
systems of punishment, 29

T

Taiwan, 18
tariffs, 19
temporal NOR, 115
Terraza, V., 60
Tesauro, G., 72

thematic global macro, vi
theory of conformity, 12
Thompson sampling, 117–119
threshold NOR, 115
time series, 143–144
tit-for-tat, 27
total distance score, 125
totalitarian systems, 20
trade barriers, 19
trade groups, 36
trade negotiations, 36, 87, 106
trade policy, 19
trade war, 88–89
transaction costs, 129
transferable utility game, 60
treatment, 100–102
Trivers, R.L., 27
Trump, 18
trust, 34, 53
Turkey, 16–17, 53
Turkmenistan, 20
type, 38–39, 78–79

U

UK, 53, 76
Ukraine, 18
Ullmann-Margalit, E., 29–30, 33–35
units of analysis, 15, 19
upper confidence bound (UCB) algorithm, 40–41, 117–118
US, 18, 76

V

van den Brink, R., 151
Vardi, M.Y., 150
Vanberg, V., 32
Veinott, A.F., 38
velocities, 86
von Wright, G.H., 96
voting, 29

W

Waltz, K.N., 15–16
Wang, Z., 72
war of attrition (WA), 74, 76–77

Watkins, C.J.C.H., 72
weighted NOR, 115
Weirich, P., 35
Weltanschauung, 15
Wittgenstein, L., 13
Woodward, J., 96
worldview, 15
Wrangham, 50
Wright, S.J., 138
Wu, C., vi

X

Xinjiang province, 18

Y

Young, T.P., 50

Z

Zellner, A.A., 99
zero-sum game, 16

www.ingramcontent.com/pod-product-compliance
Lightning Source LLC
Jackson TN
JSHW011949070125
76732JS00002B/33